Mom Says "Is"

by Howard Sullivan

Printed in the United States of America

First Printing, 2024

ISBN 979-8-89390-031-6

Library of Congress Control Number: Pending

Ordering Information: Special discounts are available on quantity purchases by bookstores, corporations, associations, and others. For details, contact the publisher at sales@braughlerbooks.com or at 937-58-BOOKS.

For questions or comments about this book, please write to info@braughlerbooks.com.

Braughler™
Books
braughlerbooks.com

TABLE OF CONTENTS

INCLUSIONS:

PREFACE

I'm a very average guy who has lived an ordinary but amazing life. I was fortunate enough or rather blessed to be given a wonderful mother and father, two siblings that I am honored and proud to call my sisters. Linda and I had three children that mean the world to us. We have twelve grandchildren and two great grandchildren and more great grandchildren on the way. The greatest accomplishment of my life was meeting my soulmate or I could say God's greatest blessing to me was creating my soulmate and bringing us together.

We are now eighty years old. We have had a marvelous life. We never dwelled on death or morbid thoughts but were busy living and making the most of life. We never discussed death or prepared for it. I think we both thought we would ride out on the same white horse. It wasn't until my soulmate, Linda, became ill, roughly nine months ago, that we even discussed whether we wanted a burial or cremation. Linda with no hesitation informed me she wanted to be buried where her mother and father were buried. Their burial place is a cemetery in Tennessee that was established in 1888. It sets at the foot of Lookout mountain, a few blocks from the Tennessee river. Many civil war battles were fought very close by and many retired confederate soldiers are entombed there.

Until Linda became ill, I don't think either one of us felt old. I know I didn't and she never expressed anything that led me to believe she didn't feel exactly the same. She often said, "I can't understand why people are depressed". I guess what I'm trying to say is we let old age slip up on us. We never stopped to dwell on the fact that this life as we know it will end. We had plenty of time to handle that when the time comes.

Linda came from a very similar background as myself, average middle income family. Her mom and dad grew up in the same town. She had an excellent home life with great parents and one sister five years older. Her mother had one sister as well and the extended family was very close, like my family. Her father came from a large family and they too were close. Linda often talked about one of her uncles that always came to rescue her if she missed the school bus or needed assistance in any way. Both our parents worked and we had a tremendous amount in common.

We lived in different school districts and never attended the same schools but were high school sweethearts.

We were raised by very loving, church going parents, from christian churches but with different denominations. Our mothers were the driving forces in our houses that made Sunday school and church a necessity. Linda maintained that tradition after our marriage.

From the day we married everything hinged around each other. Together, we could conquer anything. Nothing could really harm us because we had each other. We were best friends, lovers and soulmates. I don't think either one of us could imagine life without the other and quite frankly, never thought about it happening. This all changed on December 22nd, 2023 at 9:15 in the evening. The miracles that she with God's grace has performed since her passing are hard to explain and difficult to elaborate. I found this out shortly after her passing. Two of the nicest ladies in the neighborhood saw me walking our little dog. They had sent me a sympathy card but hadn't attended the funeral because it wasn't in the state where we now lived. They both offered their condolences and asked how I was doing. I told them it was awful but Linda had made it bearable by giving me the knowledge of knowing she was still with me. I began to attempt to tell them about the miracles she and God had shown me since her passing. I didn't get very far, I immediately recognized their lack of understanding and sensed a desire of wishing they could just continue their morning walk. I immediately stopped the attempt to tell them what had happened and thanked them for their concern.

We felt the need to tell our children and grandchildren what had transpired since Linda's passing. We sat down and wrote them a letter telling them everything, feeling it might help them in accepting God's power and mercy. Even after this letter,

Linda and God's grace continue to support and guide me. Much more has happened.

Today, the Lead Pastor at The Hope Church spoke about Peter v4:10; "Each of you should use whatever gift you have received to serve others, as faithful stewards of God's grace in its various forms". God has extended Linda and me a tremendous gift and we feel we must attempt to make this knowledge available to as many as possible. Your soul does not perish when your body stops. My sister called me a few months ago and told me about a movie she had just watched, "Heaven is for Real". It was about a pastor in Nebraska who almost lost his four year old to a ruptured appendix who began telling his parents about going to heaven and all the people he met including Jesus. I have watched it numerous times. During the movie it portrays the pastor attempting to understand the amazing knowledge the four year old gained while going through the surgery and recovery that he didn't know or learn while on earth.

I feel the pastor in Nebraska finally realized people must be seeking answers before they are ready to accept something that is totally foreign to anything we have experienced here in our physical world. Linda and God have given me the gift of everything they say in the Bible about giving us eternal life is true. If we believe God gave his only son, Jesus Christ, to cleanse our sins and accept The Holy Spirit into our souls and ask his forgiveness, He will give us eternal life in heaven. I have seen it with my own eyes and my soulmate has confirmed it. My 29 year old granddaughter has witnessed it with me. My 53 year old daughter was also witness to the multiple day miracle. Linda has done something after passing from our physical world that she could not do while with me. I don't think Linda realized I had doubts about my faith prior to passing. I had attended church since I was old enough to walk and wanted to believe that Jesus would give us everlasting life in heaven. I wanted to believe it but it was a high mountain to climb. I was a math and science major in college and studied engineering. Little in my day to day physical world supported the spiritual teachings of the Bible. As hard as I tried to make myself believe, I still had doubts. Linda and God's mercy have removed all doubts. Why wouldn't I want to share this gift with whomever would listen? My mission now is to introduce as many souls to the Savior as possible with Linda's assistance. I am certainly not a writer and really don't know where to start. I feel God and Linda will help me. If this doesn't work I'll try something else. Linda has already had a major effect on many souls since December 22nd, 2023.

I think if you ask the average person on the street if they believe in God, the large majority would say yes. However, when you start to attempt to explain the miracles you have experienced they seem afraid or uncomfortable even talking about it. I now know God gives us gifts. He is soliciting us to follow him and wants us to have everlasting life. When God gives us these remarkable gifts we need to accept them. I fear too many people look for excuses to discredit these gifts rather than accept the gift from God. I have been guilty of this most of my life. I was guilty of this practice, in this instance. Rather than being open to his miracles, I would first attempt to make them fit physically. Even though I had just seen it with my own eyes, I would search for a rational worldly explanation so the event would fit into the world I have known since birth. Life teaches us well. If you're fortunate enough to live as long as we have, you feel you know what is physically possible and what is not. In my case, I had to be hit over the head by my soulmate (repeatedly) before I would accept her intervention and existence. Linda would not relent. When I managed to ignore her initial contact with my logic of its impossibility, she would try another approach. Finally, she forced me to seek assistance from someone knowledgeable enough to explain what was happening. Thanks to the beautiful soul I married, I have seen and experienced the Lord's miracles and know anything is possible through The Father, The Son and The Holy Spirit.

I don't have many answers or facts about what we should expect when we pass over. I do know that my sweet and loving angel is watching over me and guiding me. I do know that God is a loving God. Death is not the end but a new beginning. Everything will be revealed to us in His time. We want to share the gift we have received by God's grace in its various forms.

> *P.S.: It has now been roughly seven months since Linda and I started documenting and recording God's gift to us. We are in the editing and reviewing stage of sending this whatever it is; recording of events, reveals, miracles, gained knowledge to a publisher so that the sharing could begin. We are both still here and she and God continue to guide this endeavor. I love the contact and guidance but it makes it more difficult to know when to complete this project.*

HEAVEN ON EARTH

Linda and I met in our senior year of high school. She went to a suburban county high school and I went to a large urban school. We both came from very stable loving homes. Both families were middle income. Both parents in the family worked. Linda and Howard were the youngest in their families. Linda had one older sister and Howard had two. Both were raised in christian families where church and Sunday school were attended weekly.

The mothers of both families were the driving forces behind their religious upbringing. We had many things in common.

I first saw Linda at a high school football game. I was in the stands watching the halftime show with some buddies. Linda was a majorette marching and twirling a baton during half time. She was one of several cute majorettes on the field along with her high school marching band. Linda stood out. I was struck by her beauty. She had a long ponytail and was exceptionally cute. I felt I would be reaching too high to pursue her but I did learn her name, Linda Donaldson, just in case. This occurred in the fall of our senior year.

The next time I saw Linda it was a pretty warm day. I don't remember what day of the week it was, I just remember it was lunch time and I wasn't in class. Perhaps it was a Saturday. I pulled into the local drive-in to get lunch. As I was walking into the restaurant, I looked up and I was walking straight towards the rear of a 1957 red Ford convertible with the top down. It was full of pretty girls. The girl in the far right rear seat had a long ponytail. I recognized it was Linda Donaldson. This was the side I was walking by. It was too late to change my approach and avoid the car, it would have been too obvious. I was outnumbered and outgunned. As I walked by the car, I heard a sweet girl's voice say, "Hey". I turned around and replied, "Hey". It was Linda. She asked me if I could bring her the salt. I was so surprised by the request I didn't know how to answer. I attempted to be cool and answered something like, "Sure". All the way into the restaurant I was feeling a little used or just maybe she was flirting. No, I decided I was being used. I grabbed a salt shaker from the table and returned it to Linda. I tried to act cool and asked her if there was anything else she needed as I handed her the salt shaker. She said no and thanked me. We still have that salt shaker.

Our home town opened new bowling centers during our junior and senior years of high school. They became the preferred hangouts for teenagers. One night a group of my buddies were invited to a girls slumber party at one of the girls' homes. The girls were from Linda's high school. Obviously, we jumped at the opportunity. Things were different back then. There was no physical contact involved, just a chance to meet girls from other high schools in the area. When we arrived at the home of the girl hosting the slumber party we were shocked to be hit by a barrage of pillows thrown at us when we walked in. It was clear by the reception, the girls that invited us hadn't cleared it with the girl hosting the party and most importantly her parents. This home was a long distance from the bowling alley. We had followed the girls while they went by their houses and picked up overnight clothes. I didn't know Linda was among the girls we were following but later learned we had gone by her house. When we were so rudely met at the door with the pillows we left. A few of the girls came out to apologize to us and sat in the car and talked for a while. Linda was among them. I don't recall who they were other than Linda. She sat in the back seat of my car along with a couple of her girl friends. I was totally impressed with her beauty and kindness. Even her voice was perfect, warm and sweet. She was rather quiet but seemed sincerely apologetic about the way we were treated after being invited. I still felt she was out of my class and I would be wasting my time to pursue her. This happened on a cold winter night with some icy spots on the road. After the girls went into the house, we backed out of the driveway and stopped in front of the house. One of my friends made the suggestion I should peel rubber pulling away from the house. Stupidly, I acted on his suggestion. Unfortunately, I had stopped on a patch of ice. I had planned to just peel out a little bit. When I popped the clutch, the rear tires spun on the ice very rapidly but made no noise. All of a sudden the tires spun through the ice and met the hard surface of the pavement. All we heard within the car was a loud pow in the rear of the car. I had broken the rear axle of my old 1950 chevy. The car wouldn't move. It was freezing outside and we were miles away on a lake where they were having a slumber party at a summer home. The surrounding homes were vacant for the winter. The only phone available was in the house where scores of girls were having a slumber party. I was forced to go back to the door to call for help. I couldn't get any of my friends to go with me to the door. I don't remember what I said but I had to convince them I needed to call for help. I do remember I was very embarrassed at the time. Little did I know what I said impressed Linda. She later told me I said, "Seriously, I broke my car and I need to call my dad". This was well before cell phones and the only phone was in the great room of this lake house. A house full of girls watched and listened to me tell my daddy I needed him to come miles up on the lake to pick me and my friends up. She later told me she was impressed first of all that I called my dad instead of a friend but also by the way I spoke to my father and the respect I showed him during the call.

After this meeting, Linda and I still didn't get together. I did realize she was something special and not what I expected from such a cute girl. Linda felt a little more out of my reach. I don't remember how long it was before Linda and I met again. I had a part time job at a Texaco gas station. It was a Saturday late afternoon and I had just gotten home from work. The phone rang, it was a school mate that I often bummed a ride home from school. He was dating Linda's best friend. Linda was talking to her best friend and asked her what she was doing that night. Her friend said she had a date with my school mate. Linda asked her to have him get her a date and they could double date. He gave Linda's friend a list of names he felt she might consider. It seems Linda chose me out of the list. I jumped at the chance. This started our life together. The more I learned about Linda, the more I knew this was the person I wanted to spend my life with. I had never met a gorgeous girl who was so considerate and humble. She doesn't think she is special which makes her that much more special. She isn't impressed by material things but more by how you treat people. She is real. Linda is the wisest person I know. She always makes the right decision. She can see through the forest and see the trees. We began to date regularly. My life suddenly became all about Linda. I would cut the sixth period study hall and go to her high school and pick her up so she didn't have to ride the bus and we could be together sooner.

For high school graduation, I gave Linda a nice Bulova wrist watch. It was the most expensive watch I could afford and had ever purchased for anyone in my seventeen years of life. I didn't tell anyone. At first, she wouldn't accept it. I convinced her that I was crazy about her and she was the most important thing in my life. I don't remember the exact cost but I know it was under $100.00 with tax. But when you consider, you could buy a new Chevy or Ford automobile for approximately $2,000.00 it was an expensive graduation gift for the time.

Linda had been accepted at The University of Tennessee in Knoxville. I was going to follow my sisters and attend Tennessee Tech in Cookeville, Tennessee. We both had our dorm rooms and were set to attend in the fall of 1961. The more I learned about this amazing person, the more I realized we needed to be together. I was afraid I would lose her. I knew she would have her pick of any guy she met at college. I knew who I wanted to spend my life with and I hoped she felt the same. Boy was I right. We went to our parents and told them we wanted to get married. Obviously, they reacted like any parents that had two teenagers wanting to get married would. They explained all the reasons we shouldn't and we could go ahead as planned with our college plan and continue dating as the colleges were less than sixty miles apart. I was not confident enough in myself to take that chance. I convinced Linda to postpone starting college that fall and we both got jobs. Linda went to work downtown at Kay Jewelers and I went to work at a local department store a few blocks away. We were now both eighteen and felt we were adults. Little did we know.

I was determined. I had found what I wanted in life and it was Linda Donaldson. I knew if I let her get away, I would never be truly happy. Linda is the girl I was supposed to be with. I did my best sales job on her. I pointed out we had tried to do it right and involve our families in our marriage. They were as adamant in our waiting as I was about getting married now. I could never love anyone else like I loved Linda. I finally convinced her to travel to Lafayette, Georgia to get married. We crossed state lines into Georgia and obtained our blood test. We then drove to Lafayette to be married. Georgia would allow us to be married that day if we would sign a document saying she was pregnant and that we had to get married. Linda absolutely refused to sign that document and I understood. I had pressured Linda to sleep with me for months to no avail. Both our families and upbringing had stressed you should not have sex before you married. They explained to us that if we didn't agree to sign the statement admitting she was pregnant we had to wait three days before we could get married.

We waited for three days. That was a long three days. I constantly worried that she would back out. I was so immature, I never once considered if I should back out. Three days later, November 14, 1961, we drove back to Lafayette, Georgia. The Justice of Peace would marry us right there at the courthouse. He was rather heavy and unkept wearing a plaid shirt that revealed what he had eaten for breakfast. Linda insisted we be married by a minister. They handed us a phone book and we began calling local ministers. After several calls we reached a Presbyterian minister in Lafayette. He was willing to perform the marriage in his home.

We were pleasantly surprised when we arrived at his home. It was a white cottage with white picket fence and roses growing all around the house. We commented it looked like something out of Hollywood. It was perfect. When I think about it now, it was November. How is it possible roses were all around? I don't know, perhaps it was an unusual warm fall. After all it was Georgia and I remember it being a beautiful day and comfortable temperature. Regardless, that is the picture in my memory and it is vivid. They were an elderly couple in their sixties. The wife played the piano in their living room. It was perfect. It was just like the movies. Unfortunately, we don't have a single picture. I was so immature I hadn't realized there was a fee associated with the actual ceremony and barely had enough to pay the minister. I did not have adequate funds to tip the minister. The only pictures we have of this event are in our memories and for me they are vivid. It was the single greatest event of my life. I still remember holding that sweet little soft hand and thinking, this will be the same little soft hand I will hold for the rest of my life. I have never lost that feeling.

It took a while to grow up and grasp my responsibilities. Overnight my confidence soared. Linda had chosen me. I was something special. With her by my side, I could do anything. Together, we could conquer anything that came our way. Kenny Rogers wrote a song that captured the effect Linda Donaldson had on me. He wrote and sang about our life together. The name of the song was "You Decorated My Life". He released the song back in 1979. Everytime I hear it, wonderful memories of our physical life together come flooding back.

A year later we had our first child, a boy. I was named after my father and was a junior. In honor of my father, we named him the same and he became a III. We nicknamed him Trey. We were nineteen and parents. My mother had secured me a job where she worked, DuPont. It was a factory that produced nylon for everything from hosiery to automobile tires. My mother was an inspector and only worked 8:00 AM to 4:00 PM weekdays. The plant was unlike any factory I had ever seen, and you could eat off the floor. It was so clean. They prided themselves on their safety record and it was always safety first. It was the highest paying job I could hope to find with my education, age and lack of experience. Unfortunately, most employees worked swing shifts. Seven days working 8:AM - 4:PM, seven days 4:PM - 12PM and seven days 12PM - 8:AM with a few days off between these shifts. You never could get adjusted to a shift. It was constantly changing. It disrupts virtually every aspect of your family life. You were either working or sleeping when your family was living. A year later, we had just turned twenty, we purchased our first home. At that time, you could not get a mortgage until you were twenty one years of age. Linda's mother and my father went before a judge and swore we were mature enough to pay a mortgage. It was called "Removing Your Age of Minority". Legally we were responsible for our debts!

We realized we didn't want to continue this lifestyle for the rest of our life. However, the money was good and it afforded the family a certain level of comfort. We decided I should go back to school. I enrolled at the local private college. It was very expensive compared to the state colleges but it was the only college in town. DuPont had a program for those employees wanting to further their education. They would pay your college tuition and pay for all books as long as you maintained a "B" average. The college had a pretty extensive night school program and in time I was able to schedule enough hours to be considered a full load or 12 hours of credits per semester. Obviously, the 4:PM to 12:PM shift was a huge problem on school nights. I was constantly having to swap out with other employees to make classes. We did this year round for six and a half years. Linda did everything she could to make life easier. Often she ran my bath water so I could sleep a little longer after working two shifts in a row in order to make my classes. We realized that staying with DuPont, I would be promoted to management but it would be the same swing shift lifestyle. We were ready to live on the same time schedule as the rest of our friends and family.

We chose to go to work with Colgate-Palmolive Company. We took a sales position calling on both retail and wholesale accounts. I say we because it was our career. I couldn't have done it without Linda's total support. Colgate moved us seven times over the next twenty three years. When they offered me a promotion we sat down and discussed it. If Linda felt it was good for our career and family she would simply ask when do we move. The company took care of the move and Linda took care of everything else; new church, new schools, new doctors and dentist. All I had to do was go to work. Linda was and is amazing. We got the promotions.

We had three children, two boys and a girl. The first boy we named after my father, the second boy we named after her father (Linda is a daddy's girl.) and the daughter we named after Linda's mother. Each of our children had four children of their own and brought us twelve grandchildren. To date, we have two great grandchildren with more on the way.

Linda and I are soulmates. Everything in our lives revolved around each other. I was totally aware I was the luckiest man on

God's green earth. Over the years we had terrible days like the loss of our parents and loved ones but together we could handle it. Linda always had my back and I always had hers. I adore everything about her. I strive to be more like her. Linda doesn't have a vindictive thought about her. She lived her life as God intended us to. She was a living witness for the glory of God, an angel on earth, my angel.

Our last move with Colgate was to Cincinnati, Ohio. The largest grocery chain in the country is located there and it is reasonably close to Tennessee and extended family. We loved Cincinnati. It was a well kept secret to us. It had many old neighborhoods where old homes and big trees were treasured. We had always bought new or relatively new homes for their resale opportunity as it seemed like we were constantly moving. Real estate was much less expensive in Cincinnati than it was in Chicago, where we had moved from. To avoid paying taxes on the sale of our house in Chicago, we needed to reinvest in a comparably priced home in Cincinnati. Against Linda's wishes, the kids and I chose this large tudor home on a main street that was built in 1918. She was right but she eventually gave in and we settled into a wonderful life in our old home. We spent the next thirty something years shopping and filling up this wonderful house with antique treasures we found together. We hosted numerous extended family Thanksgivings and holidays. Our daughter was married and had her reception at this house. One of our granddaughters was born in that house.

We retired from Colgate when Linda and I were fifty. The home office for Colgate was in New York. We didn't want to live in New York. I took early retirement and started our own business. Linda went into real estate. We never made as much money as we had at Colgate but we loved our life together. It would take a lifetime to recount all the wonderful memories we had together. Most times me being too ambitious in most everything we attempted and Linda jumping in to save the day. Our most cherished times were spent just the two of us together. It didn't matter when or where as long as we were together. Our driving vacations and discovering new places were special but so were the simple days spent at home working in our gardens just enjoying life together. We developed a tradition during our retirement. On a typical day, our second cup of coffee included a friendly game of rummy in our sunroom. It was what followed breakfast, just sitting together in the room enjoying each oth-er's presence. This is where we solved all the world's problems and where we determined what we were going to do that day, always together, her reading her magazines and me reading my magazines. This alone describes heaven for me. Heaven can't be heaven unless it includes Linda and me together. It doesn't seem possible I was fortunate enough to not only meet Linda but for us to fall in love and spend our lives together. That God gave me the wisdom to recognize what an amazing and wonderful being Linda "is".

But when you stop and reflect, in the big scheme of things, a lifetime is just a flash in time. In my case, a wonderful flash thanks to my soulmate and the grace of God. What we are talking about here, can't be measured in time. Time has no place in eternity. God doesn't promise us more time in Heaven. He promises us eternity in Heaven.

LINDA AND HOWARD'S LAST PHYSICAL YEAR

Let us begin by telling you the events that led up to our last year of being physically together. We had no real physical ailments for the first 59 years of our lives. I fell off a ladder playing in the back yard and managed to break both arms at the same time when I was in sixth grade and contacted ringworm at the Saturday movie matinee. Linda had gone to sleep under a tanning lamp as a teenager and received a major sunburn. We both recovered and other than an occasional cold or a case of poison ivy we both led a pretty healthy life.

Obviously, Linda bore the discomfort and pain of bearing three children. One of these children, the middle child Glen, was virtually natural childbirth. She woke me at 7:30 or 8:00 AM in the morning and told me we should start for the hospital. Our first house, which we were still in, was a small ranch house sitting on five acres. I was a city boy and had always wanted land and to live in the country. Linda had lived on numerous farms and grew up in the country and had her own horse. When we were first starting out, rather than buy us a decent stove, I paid $20.00 for a second hand old used stove and bought myself a $500.00 Tennessee Walking Horse. Our first son, Trey, had taken twenty seven hours to deliver. I felt we had plenty of time. My horse was out in the pasture. I went out and caught him and put him in the barn and fed him. I knew we would be gone for a while. I stopped and got gas and Linda was saying, I think we need to hurry. I checked her into the hospital at 10:10 AM as they took Linda upstairs to delivery. I was going to school at the time and went back to my car to get my school books to study while I settled down for a long wait. In those days, the father was not allowed to be with the mother in delivery. I took my books to the waiting room and it was quite large and full of weary guys that had obviously been there for some time. There was only one open chair in the waiting room. Evidently, this chair was vacant because the person sitting in this chair had just become a father. I sat down in the chair and opened the book I was going to study. As soon as I opened the book, the phone rang. It was right beside me. I answered the phone and the person on the other end said, "Mr. Sullivan please." I answered, "This is he." They responded, "You're the father of a fine baby boy, the doctor will meet you in front of delivery in the hall." As I hurried out of the room, I heard the remaining guys in the room scrambling to get my chair as the last two fathers evidently had been sitting in that chair. It was 11:11 AM when Glen was born. Linda had a natural childbirth. He was breach, but everything was fine. Our third child, Holly, went back to Linda's old schedule. I got her to the hospital right away but they sent me home because she went out of labor around midnight. They told me they would induce labor in the morning. I just got home and the phone rang at 2:AM and they told me to hurry because she had started labor on her own. I didn't make it back in time.

As for my ailments, I had a bout with kidney stones and gallbladder stones, passed the kidney stones had gallbladder removed. At the age of 59, I had a heart attack and double by-pass heart surgery. This was accompanied with a defibrillator a year later. Linda woke me up roughly at age 70 and said take me to the emergency room. She was diagnosed with rheumatoid arthritis. Linda went through several different medications to attempt to control flare ups from the arthritis. They steadily became stronger and stronger until she ended up on biologic medication. She tried several different infusion biologics and shots until she ended up on a pill medication called Xeljanz XR. Four years ago, Linda had a bad UTI infection. She was prescribed an antibiotic to treat the infection. Linda became very confused and I thought she was losing her mind. Everyone said the confusion was caused by the combination of the infection and the antibiotics. It took Linda a long time to get over the confusion.

The next appointment with her rheumatologist, he announced he was taking her off Xeljanz. I questioned why, as she isn't having any flare ups. He informed me the medication had been linked to strokes. Today, he can't prescribe this medication to anyone over 40 years of age. I am now convinced that the confusion everyone thought was caused by the UTI was due to a stroke.

We downsized from our large home to a much smaller condo in January of 2022. During this move, I injured myself twice.

Once when I was running out to the detached garage to get a box, in the dark, and stepped on a frozen gumball, prickly seed from a gum tree. I broke my left foot and was placed in a boot. The other injury was a hernia sustained when I reached over the foyer table to pack a large fifty pound mirror. I went to my primary doctor and he said it was a small hernia and unless it starts bothering me I don't need to do anything.

Fast forward to 2023, Linda had been hit with three UTI's and had been hospitalized three times primarily because she wasn't hydrating enough. My hernia had steadily gotten worse. I went to see a surgeon and he scheduled an operation to repair the hernia. Shortly after scheduling the operation I was walking our little dog and I experienced a funny feeling in my arms. We called my cardiologist and went in for a stress test. He didn't like the test and then performed an angiogram in April of 2023. The result was he placed two stints in my old original bypass arteries. All this was going on at the same time. This brought back some of the confusion but we both recovered. My hernia surgery was postponed because of me being placed on a blood thinner for six months, due to the stints.

My mothers side of the family organized a family reunion in Wilmington, NC. The reunion took place on Father's Day weekend which fell on June 18th. We almost didn't go because Linda was just recovering from her latest UTI and all the medical issues. We decided to go at the last minute. Linda did great. Her clarity returned and she was her old self, cutting up with my sisters and we had a wonderful time. Of the forty attendees, eighteen contracted Covid. We all thought that Covid had waned and Linda was out of danger, we feared her contracting it with her immune system compromised by the biologic infusions she was getting for her rheumatoid arthritis.

We returned from North Carolina realizing that a couple of the attendees showed signs of illness but it had not been officially diagnosed as Covid. Within a day the news was they had Covid. Within the first week, I came down with Covid but Linda felt fine. I was down and in bed for three days. The fourth day I was fine. Linda was still fine. Linda's birthday is June 28th, she turned eighty. My baby was eighty. I went out and got her all the fixings for a big birthday. The day before her birthday she became sick. I tested her and she proved positive to Covid. Obviously, the party was canceled. Covid hit her very hard. She made no sense to me and I couldn't even give her the Covid test because she objected so strongly. I became scared on June 30th and called the non-emergency ambulance. The last thing she did prior to going to the hospital was walk to the bathroom.

Linda was very disoriented when we checked in the hospital. The doctor in charge visited her and prescribed Paxlovid, a five day medication to lessen the effects of covid.The doctor visited her on Monday morning and was surprised at how Linda had improved in just one day. He visited again on Tuesday and commented he may release her on Wednesday but wanted her to go to a rehab facility. She was transferred to a so-called rehab center by ambulance on Wednesday afternoon.

Linda was quarantined at the end of one of the facility's hallways until the following Monday, 4 1/2 days. They placed her on a Hoyer lift, which would not fit through the bathroom door. When she pushed her call button to go to the restroom, they took forever to respond. Looking back on it, we would never recommend anyone go to a so-called rehab center. If they are all administered like the one they sent us to, they are a scam against medicare. We waited as long as eight hours and fifteen minutes for one of the aids to respond to the call button. When someone finally responded and we complained, the aid responded that it wasn't her section, she just saw the light was on. It wasn't just Linda that was ignored. Down the hall from Linda, I could hear a faint little voice saying, "Help me". Turns out the voice was coming from a sweet 93 year old woman that just needed water. Her name was Ruth and I helped her every time I heard her calling. She was pushing her button but no one was responding.

My son and his wife were visiting Linda that Monday evening. I took the opportunity to go home and take care of our little dog. My son called and said he was very concerned with his mom's condition. He had the nurse check her vital signs and they were not good. They called the ambulance and she was rushed back to the hospital. The emergency doctor told us it was Covid rebound. If the Paxlovid medication doesn't totally knock it out, it comes back with a vengeance. It was at this time the doctors asked me if Linda had ever been diagnosed with heart arrhythmia. I told them no. They informed me she now had it, I suppose a result of covid. Again, she recovered fairly quickly and the same doctor started talking about releasing her to the rehab center. I informed him I didn't want to take her back to the same rehab center. We contacted every other so-called rehab center and no one else would take a Covid patient. I did manage to keep her at the hospital for nine days this time. Here is where I made a bad mistake. Linda had been forced to wear disposable underwear or Depends for seventeen days. The medical personnel had forced her to become incontinent. Her last act at home had been to walk to the bathroom. By keeping her off her feet and using the Hoyer lift for seventeen days and the combination of not being able to take her arthritis medication due to covid, she had difficulty standing on her own. I later discovered the Hoyer lift was employed because the nurses felt she might fall although she never had. After seventeen days of being off her feet she didn't have the strength to stand on her own. I should have never allowed her to go back to the rehab (nursing home) center. If I had it to do over, I would get in-home care to help me and take her straight home.

Early on at the nursing home, we noticed Linda had a red spot at the base of her spine on her bottom. The nursing home staff immediately jumped in and said they would take care of it. They put some ointment on the area and placed a large bandage over it. We knew nothing about bed sores. We were getting her up daily and taking her for walks in her wheelchair. Linda never complained but began to refuse to attempt to stand. We were never allowed to see the bed sore again while we were at the nursing home. Every time they went to change the bandage, I was ushered out of the room. I thought I was doing the right thing for Linda's privacy as the staff had forced her to be incontinent and they had to clean her up when changing the bandage.

With no warning I was told medicare would no longer pay for Linda to stay at the so-called rehab center. It was going to cost $12,000.00 per month to keep her there. Since they were pathetic and inept in their care of Linda, at the advice of a family friend and RN, I took her home under the care of hospice. She explained that hospice is not what everyone thinks that you are not on death's doorstep and just to keep you comfortable until you pass. I believed this and hired a wonderful in-home caregiving company for ten hours a day, seven days a week care.

We took Linda home on the first of August. The first time my caregivers got a look at the bed sore they called me in to see for myself. We couldn't imagine the damage the nursing home had allowed to occur without taking action. I couldn't imagine the pain Linda must have endured to get in this condition. The bed sore was a large golf ball size hole that went all the way to her spine. Hospice jumped in and said they would handle it and treat it with an ointment, Medi-Honey. My in-home caregivers took me aside and told me the only way Linda would survive and heal this bed sore was through a wound center. The wound needed to be cleaned out and the dead flesh removed from the wound. The wound would never heal properly without the surgery. Hospice refused to allow her to go to a wound center; they wanted to just continue their ointment therapy with no surgery.

I took her out of hospice care and took her to the best wound center in Cincinnati. Our friend and nurse knew the surgeon personally and got us an appointment right away. We all knew Linda had an uphill battle to recover. With all the UTI's and now covid, she hadn't been able to take her rheumatoid arthritis medication. This was a major reason she didn't want to stand and walk. The pain and laying in bed for six weeks had taken their toll on her. She was amazing. She soldiered on, never complaining and smiling.

On the day of Linda's appointment with the surgeon, my son and his wife along with her in-home caregiver accompanied me. They would only allow two of us in the examination room. My son and I were with Linda during the examination. The doctor did not have good news for us. Basically, he told us that the wound was too advanced for him to help her. Even if he attempted the surgery, Linda with her weakened condition, would not survive the surgery. He told us to take her home and keep her comfortable, there was nothing he could do. I was told to take my baby girl home and keep her comfortable. This couldn't be. I was going to lose the love of my life to a neglected bed sore. The doctor didn't know Linda.

I took Linda home and we continued the medi-honey treatment with my in-home caregiver, Natasha. She was wonderful. Natasha took wonderful care of Linda. She never let the wound go uncared for. She was constantly changing and cleaning the wound. Due to the location of the wound, keeping it clean was imperative to Linda healing. Linda and Natasha became very close. Natasha came everyday, seven days a week. Never a day off. Natasha was raised by her father. I gathered she was not close to her mother. Linda's progress was amazing under the care of Natasha. The dead tissue was gone and new tissue began to appear. We took pictures of the wound and sent them to the surgeon's office. He was amazed by her improvement. He scheduled a debridement surgery to clean out the wound. Linda came through it in flying colors.

They did find bad bacteria in the wound and placed Linda on a sixty day antibiotic treatment.

Linda's attitude was unbelievable. She took everything in stride. She seldom complained and made the best of her situation. Her appetite was great. As long as we kept her hydrated, she was fine. Linda had now been off her feet and virtually in bed since June 30th and it was December 18th, five months and going on three weeks. She had an appointment with her wound center surgeon on Monday, December 18th, 2023. She was amazed at her progress and improvement of her wound. Linda had completed six weeks of antibiotic treatment. The doctor scheduled a second and hopefully final surgery to cap the wound so it could totally heal. Linda and her doctor had a most encouraging conversation about her progress and the outlook for her future.

Due to my two stents placed back in April, my hernia operation had finally taken place on December 5th, thirteen days prior to Linda's December 18th appointment. I was limited to picking up ten pounds and warned to be careful. During getting Linda in the car, Natasha and my granddaughter had almost dropped her. The wheelchair was in their way and I moved it to the back of the SUV and put it in the rear. It was much heavier than I should have lifted. I felt a sharp pain where the surgery was performed. I was certain I had done damage. I called my hernia doctor and he got me in that Wednesday.

More good news! My hernia was fine. Linda had the most positive appointment possible with her wound doctor and I hadn't damaged my hernia when loading the wheelchair. After everything piled on top of her she was fighting through it and was actually getting better. Linda was a super woman. My son Glen, had never offered negative comments about his mother's prognosis, just positive support. With this positive news, he confessed to me he didn't see how mom could possibly survive with everything thrown at her. He thought I was simply unable to face reality and couldn't face the fact that I was losing her. He now believed like me, Linda was going to beat this too. On top of everything thrown at her she will beat it.

My neighbor called Thursday night and asked how Linda was doing. I told him the good news. She is having her surgery in a couple of weeks to totally heal the wound. We can then resume her arthritis medication and get her back on her feet. Everything was coming up roses. My Linda was unstoppable. Secretly, I didn't know how she was doing it. I couldn't have done it. I was confined to bed for a week once with a gall bladder and was climbing the walls. My tolerance to being confined to bed was non-existent. I realized Linda was the strength in our marriage. Not only was she the strength but the wisdom. She always had the right approach and answers to challenges in our lives.

What a wonderful turn around in our lives. We have come through a very challenging year and the future looks bright. We have several more good years together. Linda is going to be back on her feet and we can find that winter home further south. Many more memories to look forward to. Life is good. We still have problems in the extended family but we do have time to work on them. Everything is working out. I slept great that Thursday night. Thanks to God, my angel was staying with me.

DECEMBER 22ND, 2023

December 22nd, 2023 was a Friday. It started like most other days over the past five months but with a good deal more optimism. Natasha showed up as usual and bathed Linda and fixed her hair. I made Linda's breakfast and boiled eggs for us all. Linda had her usual robust breakfast of yogurt, boiled egg, cinnamon toast and jelly, oatmeal, cranberry juice and a thirty graham protein chocolate drink. Her appetite was super. Linda enjoyed her food very much but maintained her weight of 116 pounds. Linda took her time eating as it was one of her few pleasures at this time. She and Natasha would watch television and they were constantly talking. As I said before, they became close and friends. I had walked our little dog and cleaned up the kitchen. Olivia, our granddaughter who lived with us, had gone to work. By the time all this had taken place it was pushing 11:00AM.

My neighbor called and inquired about Linda. I told him all the good news we had received that week from all our doctors. I have a couple of fish tanks that we had brought from our old house. I busied myself taking care of the fish, walking the dog and vacuuming. It was a very normal day. Natasha fed Linda her lunch rather late, starting around two. As usual, Linda took her time while watching television. She ate, among other things, a full can of Progresso Broccoli Cheese soup. It is her favorite. It was pushing four o'clock by the time she finished lunch.

I walked into the bedroom and she looked precious. She was sitting halfway up in her hospital bed. She rolled her eyes at me and I said, "You look good enough to eat. I might just eat you up". She just looked at me with her cute little smile. To me, she looked as cute as the little girl I had married 62 years before. I said, "I'm going to get all your kisses. Can I have all your kisses". I leaned over her and started to kiss her all over her cheeks, nose and ears and heard her softly say, "Sure".

Natasha left at six o'clock. Linda was taking a nap. I walked the dog and when I came back she was still sleeping peacefully. It was now about 6:30. Since she had finished her lunch so late I decided to let her sleep as it wasn't unusual for her to eat after eight. I went into the den and turned the television on. I obviously dozed off. The next sound I heard was Olivia coming home from work. It was after eight o'clock and Olivia was already upstairs in her room. As usual these days, when I first woke up, I headed to the restroom. I hollered up to Olivia to inquire if she had fed Linda. She was now coming down the stairs and I met her as I was walking into the powder room. She said no she hadn't fed her because she was sleeping.

When I came out of the bathroom, Olivia was coming out of our bedroom telling me, "Grammy won't wake up". I shouted for her to call 911 and ran into the bedroom. Linda was lying just like I had left her when I was getting all her kisses. She was limber and warm but not responding to me talking to her and asking her to wake up. By this time, Olivia walked into the room while talking to 911. They were telling her an ambulance was on its way and instructing her on how to perform CPR. It dawned on me that my neighbor right across the driveway was a nurse for Christ Hospital. I ran to her door and kept ringing the bell until she came to the door. When she appeared at the door I asked her if she could perform CPR. As I got these words out of my mouth a police car pulled into our driveway followed by paramedics. The hospital is less than two miles away and they were there in record speed.

The paramedics came in and ushered us out of the bedroom. By this time my son and his wife had gotten there from four miles away. I didn't remember who called them. They told me I had called around 8:45 PM and said, "I've lost her". They said they dropped everything and were here in less than five minutes. I remember nothing of that phone call. The lead paramedic came into the den and told us we have a weak heartbeat and they are assisting her with breathing and heartbeat. I had just felt her and knew she was going to be okay. She was going to beat this also.

We sat there talking about how much better she had been doing and how strong she was. The lead paramedic came in and gave us updates from time to time. I was scared but could not imagine her not making it.

At 9:15 PM on Friday, December 22nd, 2023, the lead paramedic came into the room and announced to us all that Linda had passed away. No! This couldn't be. He's wrong. My doll baby can't be gone. He immediately went into telling us what was going to happen. The funeral home was going to come in and take control of the body, etc. I said absolutely not. You're not taking Linda without me saying goodby and hugging and kissing her. I guess deep down I felt I could bring her back, wake her up, she couldn't be gone. I hadn't been without her for over 63 years. I couldn't imagine life without her in it and by my side.

The paramedic tried to discourage me from going to Linda. I think his words were, "We don't recommend that". I couldn't understand that statement. No way am I going to let them take my soulmate without saying goodby. I have to hold my doll baby one more time. I still couldn't comprehend she was gone from our physical world.

I walked into our bedroom and was shocked to see the paramedics had moved Linda's body onto the floor between her hospital bed and our bedroom dresser. She had a breathing tube still in her mouth. She looked tiny lying on the floor. There wasn't enough room for me to lay or sit beside her. I decided I would straddle her and walk up so I could bend over and hold her face and kiss her on the nose and forehead. When I bent down over her and reached down and held her face, I was again shocked . I had just held her and she was warm and alive. This was not my Linda. Her spirit had already left her body. I now realize why they didn't recommend attempting to hold her and say goodby.

I left the room and went back to the den. I didn't even see them take her body out. This wasn't real. I was going to wake up from this nightmare. Somebody wake me up. I don't remember much about the remainder of the night. I did see the neighbor I had talked to earlier that day standing at the end of my driveway, the neighbor I had given all the positive information concerning Linda's prognosis. As the night went on and the facts started to sink in, I felt I couldn't take it. I had lost my unyielding support. I had lost my soulmate. I simply could not go on without her. I thought, when everyone leaves, I'll join her. We were supposed to go out together. I'll simply go out in the garage and start the car and leave the garage door down. We'll be together right away. By this time it was the wee hours of the morning. I was wishing everyone would leave so we could carry out my plan of joining her. Linda let me know, I don't know how, but she let me know that is the one way we will never be together again. It's not my choice or her choice when we pass, it's God's choice.

With my plan to join her blowing up, I felt deep despair and didn't know if I could take it. The next morning my neighbor called and asked if everything was alright. He didn't know. When he was standing at the end of our driveway, he asked the police officer if everything was alright. He answered him very positively, "We have everything under control". When I told him Linda had passed he was shocked.

The unthinkable had happened. My reason for living was gone. The center of my being was gone. Why am I still here?. Life seems hollow and meaningless without Linda Donaldson with me. What good am I? I couldn't protect her. I should have done more. I should have not accepted the advice of the doctors and allowed her to go to that awful nursing home. Why was I so weak that I couldn't protect the most valuable and wonderful soul in our lives? Why didn't he take me? I'm the one with the heart condition. I'm the sinner. She is the angel on earth. She was the one that lived her life witnessing to God through the way she treated everyone. It can't be!

LINDA'S CONTACT

I didn't sleep at all for the first 2 1/2 days. It was surreal. Finally, on the third day I fell asleep on the sofa. I slept approximately two hours on that third day. I woke up feeling like Linda had been with me and had asked for my help. This was a godsend based on my frame of mind. I had something to think about other than Linda being gone. I felt I had been with her because I had that warm feeling I only get from Linda. I get it when I see her, touch her or hear her voice. I had been with Linda.

Linda's request was that she needed help with two people. She let me know she didn't do two things she meant to do before passing. One I understood immediately, the other was a complete surprise. She told me I must take a different approach with the first person and reminded me of my own mortality, I need to do it now. The second unfulfilled task she had meant to perform was simply say she forgave them and loved them. My baby needed my help. I knew what to do. For the second request, I took out a note card and told them Linda forgives you and loves you. The other task would take longer.

I only saw Linda tremble uncontrollably three times in our 63 years together. One was when her uncle called to inform her that her father had passed away suddenly from a heart attack. The other two times involved the person she was hurt by and was now asking me to relay she forgives them.

Linda has forgiven them and I feel she doesn't want me to dwell on this event in our life. I know it is one of the low points in her life. It deprived her of many rich moments and memories with people she loved. It was a misunderstanding that should have never affected our lives. This contact and Linda's forgiveness towards those that had broken her heart gave me great relief and comfort. It voided a request she had made to me while living. This was the precious Linda I had spent my life with. I knew she was with God.

I wasn't really sleeping. I think I was passing out from exhaustion. My son Glen, took control of Linda's arrangements. He did it all. I wasn't functioning very well. The funeral home was transporting Linda's body to Chattanooga. Because of the holidays, the first opportunity for a service was January 2nd, 2024. I needed to put something in writing for this memorial service in Chattanooga. I needed something to honor this angel I had spent over 63 years with. I would sleep for a short period and get up and work on Linda's eulogy. I had recently purchased a MacBook and had never used it to do anything but shop online, mostly for medical supplies for Linda. I had used google docs on my other computer and my granddaughter brought it up for me to write the eulogy.

When I started, I could not think. I sat there for a long period before something came to me to write. Finally, it came to me that you have to tell them who you're talking about. I felt I was getting help because I was so distraught and could not think. I wrote something like we are here to celebrate the life of and spelled out her entire name; first name, middle name, maiden name and surname. A little line popped up perpendicular to the line I was writing on with a little flag at the top of it. I had never seen anything like this while I was writing before. I moved my mouse over the flag and a little green box popped up with the name Linda Sullivan in it. It was a green rectangular box with white lettering inside. For a split second I thought, "Oh my God it's Linda". Then my physical logic took over, no that's not possible. Maybe, that is what I named the document. Perhaps, this is something exclusive to Mac or Apple products. I rationalized what had just happened and made it fit into my worldly world. At the time I didn't realize I hadn't named the document, or maybe I had just written her name in the first line and that was why the box popped up with Linda's name in it. I ignored the flag and eventually went on to the next line. As I was halfway through the next sentence, poof, the first line totally disappeared. I could not understand what just happened. Again, I sat there a long time attempting to understand what just happened. All I had written was Linda's full name and what we were there for. I hadn't highlighted it and hit back space. It slowly came to me that Linda never liked her middle name. She never used it. She always signed her name Linda Sullivan or Linda D Sullivan. I retyped the first sentence leaving out the middle name and no little flag appeared. I still didn't make the connection. I was aware

I was operating on empty. I was very sleep deprived and aware my thought process was slow. However, I did get the feeling she was helping. We were doing it together.

I worked on this document every waking hour. Day and night, time wasn't a factor. I did see the little flags from time to time and concentrated on what I just wrote. Sometimes I changed it and sometimes I ignored them. It was going very slow. On the third or fourth day of working on the eulogy, I was writing about our elopement. Little flags were popping up all over the place. I ignored them and continued to type. All of a sudden, Poof! The entire document disappeared. It was gone. Three or four days of attempting to write Linda's eulogy was lost. It was four o'clock in the morning. I needed help from my computer and phone expert, Olivia, my granddaughter. I went into the room where she was sleeping and woke her up. I didn't turn the light on but the computer screen put out enough light for her to see. She didn't get out of bed and placed the computer on her stomach and informed me it wasn't gone and returned the document to the screen exactly where I was when it disappeared. I thanked her and went back to my spot on the bar in the kitchen where I was working. I was so relieved. I had not lost it. When I sat down to continue, the little flags were still there. The computer wouldn't let me type or backup. It was locked. I sat there several minutes trying to figure out why it wouldn't work. After about fifteen minutes I was forced to go back and wake Olivia again. I could tell she was getting a little annoyed and took the computer and laid it on her chest. I could see her face from the light from the computer screen. I saw her eyes begin to get larger. She began to sit up and said, "It's Grammy". She said it a couple of times, "It's Grammy". I said something like, "what!". I began to put it together. When I first saw the little flags with the little green rectangle that popped up with Linda Sullivan's name in white lettering, I thought, is this Linda? I had dismissed it and attempted to rationalize it away and accepted these things as my lack of knowledge of an Apple computer. I began to understand that it was Linda revealing herself to me. Olivia jumped out of bed and began to jump up and down and shout "It's grammy". She took the computer back to the bar and set it up and began to run the mouse over the little flags. They all popped up with boxes that were green with white writing saying Linda Sullivan. Olivia explained to me that these little flags indicate you are collaborating with someone on this document. She said if you were collaborating with more than one each person would have their own color. You had to hit me over the head with it before I knew she was helping me. I felt it but with all the signs I was still too ignorant to realize what Linda was doing. She had to make the whole document disappear so Olivia would explain to me she was helping.

We screamed and cried with joy that Linda's soul was not dead. I felt I had been given new life. I could breathe. A massive weight had been lifted off me. She had come back to let me know, your spirit doesn't die. After we had awakened the entire family and everyone went back to bed, I went back to my document. I was flying now, I knew Linda was helping. I was aware Linda is not gone from me. My spirit was soaring. She had done it, she had done the impossible. Thoughts were flowing. About twenty or thirty minutes later, my daughter walked into the kitchen. She was on the other side of the bar and could only see the back of the computer. See walked in and said, "Mom says is". I didn't understand. I told her that makes no sense to me. She just kept saying, "Mom says is". She then said mom says you typed, "Linda was my soulmate". Mom says she is your soulmate. I scanned up the document a few paragraphs and there it was. I had typed, "Linda was my soulmate". There on the line was a little flag sticking up. I went into the line and changed "was" to "is" and the little flag disappeared. Linda was on the job. Olivia and I didn't go back and proofread the document but Linda did, she turned to our daughter so she could make the corrections. Again, proof Linda was with me and actively assisting me in this event. I wanted to shout to the world, "She's not gone", "all is not lost". It began to dawn on me that what the scriptures of the Bible teach is real. It's all true. Hope and joy overtook me completely. I still have my doll baby.

I have thought a great deal about the gift God has given us and how Linda has come back to let me know your soul doesn't perish when you pass over. I don't think Linda realized I had doubts about heaven and the afterlife. Just like Linda, I had attended church since I can remember. I attended church and Sunday school, Vacation Bible School, etc. I wanted to believe but deep down I had doubts. I was a math and science major in school and studied engineering in college. The teaching of the Bible just didn't match up with our physical world. From the moment we gain consciousness as a baby we learn the rules of the physical world. How are these things possible? The Bible was written by men. I wanted to believe. I hoped there was an afterlife and heaven. Linda, through the grace of God, was allowed to show me that your soul does not die when you pass. I have included a copy of this eulogy we wrote at the back of the book.

Linda continued to come to me while I slept. Each time it was accompanied with that same warm sensation that only Linda could give. I was much more receptive and alert to her contacts. It made her physical absence bearable. She was able to lessen the grief and make it bearable by knowing we would be together again. With the eulogy in hand, I traveled to Tennessee along with my granddaughter and our little dog, Billy. Linda was very close to Billy and he was always close to her. I was concerned that I couldn't do her memory justice at her service. Every time I attempted to read it to family members, I would break down and become a blubbering mess. On the morning of her service Linda came to me. I was in the shower thinking, I'll give a copy of the eulogy to the minister, just in case I break down. Linda came to me in the shower. Linda conveyed to me very clearly, "You can do it. Just read it like you're reading it to me". Once again, Linda had my back. She gave me the strength and confidence to honor my soulmate, the woman of my dreams. The most important person in my life was with me. I was telling her how grateful I was that she chose to spend her life with me. I was the luckiest man to spend my life with one of God's greatest creations, truly, an angel on earth. Later that morning, when I stood in front of the chapel I was totally aware of the honor God was bestowing upon me. He was allowing a wretch like me to honor one of his greatest creations. It was one of the most difficult and yet rewarding things I have ever done in my life. Linda had my back, just like she had all our lives. Everytime the emotion of the words overpowered me, she would have me pause and gather my emotions before reading the next line. How could you help but adore her? Even after passing over, she was still putting me first. Looking out for me, and helping me carry the load. I love her with all my being and I love God with all my being for creating her and allowing our souls to meet.

The burial plots we had purchased roughly nine months prior were not ready due to uncontrollable weather, and it being a new section of the cemetery. The funeral home said they would hold the body until the plots were available. This has become a common practice. Many funerals were postponed for long periods of time during the early stages of covid. We returned to Ohio; Olivia, Billy, myself and Linda. Linda had been with us while we wrote the eulogy in Cincinnati. Linda had been with us in Chattanooga while we stayed at my sisters and during her life celebration. She was with us as we drove back to Cincinnati. I was becoming confident she would be with me everywhere I went, just like she was when we were living together. We would go back to Tennessee when the burial plots became available. This would allow the family to contact those we were unable to reach for her memorial service due to the holidays. I could do this. Linda was with me and together by God's grace, we were unstoppable. We had work to do.

LINDA'S GUIDANCE

Linda continued to come to me while I slept. Always, with the warmth that only Linda could give me and left with clarity and understanding of her message. Almost immediately after we returned from Tennessee, I woke with the knowledge I needed to get back in church. Linda with the grace of God and Jesus Christ had shown me without question, your soul doesn't perish when your body does. Your spirit lives on. Linda was telling me my soul needed more knowledge and understanding and I could gain this best with God's people through God's word.

I told Glen and Susie, my second son and his wife, I wanted to start going back to church. I had been somewhat of a roadblock to Linda in keeping us in church and bible study. I strongly feel Linda now knows everything God wants her to know. She knew I had doubts and had not accepted Jesus Christ as my savior. She knew I couldn't just accept him 80% or 90-95%. I had to accept him totally as my Savior.

Glen and Susie told me about two local churches about four miles from our home. They were across the street from each other and good sized congregations, the Hope Church and the Christ Church. Glen seemed to prefer The Christ Church or was just more familiar with it because he had neighbors that attended it. Regardless, we decided to attend the Christ Church. I hadn't been to either church. I mistakenly turned into the Hope Church. I was forced to turn around and go across the street to Christ Church.

As I was maneuvering to turn around, something or some-one was telling me, this is where you're meant to be. This was no mistaken turn, this is where you belong. I needed to go to Hope Church but Glen and Susie were meeting us across the street. I enjoyed the service at Christ Church but it didn't really answer any questions for me. Glen was pleased with the service and minister. I still felt the other church was calling me. I told everyone I would like to try Hope Church and they agreed.

We all went to Hope Church the next week. It was amazing. I immediately knew, this is where I belong. I feel like Linda with the grace of God, Jesus Christ and the Holy Spirit led me to that particular church, to hear that sermon from that amaz-ing minister. We were all raw because it was so close to Linda's passing but so were we the previous week. The minister prefaced the sermon with a statement that the next five to seven minutes from the Bible changed his life (John 14). It was scripture about the last supper when Jesus is to be crucified the next day and the disciples are wanting to go with him. Jesus tells them that they can't go with him because they have much more work on earth to be done. It is God's will when we leave this earth not man's. Jesus tells them they will do much more than him here on earth.

The disciples question him on how are we to do this if you are gone. Jesus tells them the Lord will send them the comforter or Holy Spirit to guide them. Jesus goes on to tell them the Holy Spirit can't guide them or help unless you let him into your soul. This is the part I didn't recognize or understand. I had never understood the necessity of letting the Holy Spirit into your soul.

This was it. This was the knowledge Linda knew I needed to gain. Just like the disciples wanted to join Jesus when he passed over, I wanted to join Linda when she passed over. It is difficult to explain. Right there, right at that moment, God was offering me the Comforter, the Holy Spirit to guide and comfort me while fulfilling God's will here on earth. I had been called by my Lord and Savior. He needed me to fulfill his will on earth. I lept at the chance to serve God. How could I not after all he had done for me. I opened my heart and soul to the Holy Spirit and God's Grace came rushing in.

I had never experienced this feeling before. It was like a warm and calming wash came over all of me. Clarity like I had never experienced before. God's word and teachings were not restricting to your life but just the opposite. It wasn't what you can't do but the expansive things you could do. With the Holy Spirit guiding your life, you won't even think about doing evil things but rather concentrate on all the good we can do in this world. Our job here on earth is to witness God's love and mercy through our actions and how we treat our fellow man. To be a disciple of God's word and teachings and bring as many souls as possible to God and Jesus Christ and away from the dark one. I pray to God to give me the wisdom to best perform my mission. I couldn't wait to discover what God called on me to do.

On the night of February 13th, 2024, Linda came to me overnight. I woke with the knowledge that Linda and I should tell our grandchildren about the gift God had given us. We wanted everyone in our family to join us in heaven when they passed on. We wanted to help in any way and every way we could. What better way than to tell them about God's gift to us. I am including a copy of this letter we wrote to our twelve grandchildren. We decided to make twelve copies and give four copies to each of our children as each family consisted of four grandchildren. The parents could then decide when and if the appropriate time to distribute the letter as there was a wide range of ages. Our reasoning was, how much easier it would have been for us to accept the presence of God and the teaching of the Bible had our grandparents shared their contacts with loved ones that passed on.

The Hope Church ironically started a thirteen week Grief Share seminar on Monday nights the second week I attended. The group that signed up were eleven women and five men. That included the leader of the seminar and his wife. Both of them had lost their spouses and met at Hope. As was the custom at this seminar, everyone talked and was given time to talk about their loss and anything else they wanted to share. Starting the first week, I asked if any of their loved ones had come back to let them know everything was alright. Of the other fifteen participants, none responded. I think it was the fourth or fifth week I had asked this same question each week, and no one responded. I decided to share with the group God's gift of Linda's contact and continued guidance. At the end of this meeting, virtually the entire class was standing in front of me. One woman in particular stood out. She told me she had heard me ask the question each week. Her husband, Mike, had been silent with no contact. She said that after the previous Grief Share meeting she went home and cried and asked Mike, "Why haven't you let me know you're okay"? She then showed me her cell phone. On her phone was a picture of a leaf on her front porch shaped into a perfect heart. She told me the wind was blowing but didn't move the leaf and in the picture it was in the center of the porch and positioned directly towards the front door. Later that week, she said she was eating out with a girlfriend. It was mid-winter and cold outside. As they walked to the front door, she noticed a flower basket hanging by the sidewalk. They were empty due to the time of year. A cardinal flew up and landed in one of the baskets, she walked over to it and it didn't fly away.

A few weeks later my sister called and recommended I watch a movie, "Heaven is for Real". It was on Prime video. It was about a young minister in Nebraska, who almost loses his four year old son from a ruptured appendix. He survives and begins saying he went to heaven and met Jesus and past relatives that were dead before his birth. As soon as I hung up, I started watching the movie and became so engrossed in the movie I lost track of time. Just as the movie was ending, the phone rang. It was my eldest son, Trey. He said, "Oh, I just realized it was Monday and didn't think you would be home".

I looked at the clock and my Grief Share meeting had already started. I went to the Grief Share meeting the next week and people were saying, "I missed you last week, did you go back to Tennessee, etc.". When it came my turn to talk, I confessed what had happened. I had become so engrossed in the movie I missed the meeting. I highly recommended the movie and was surprised to discover, of the sixteen seminar attendees, only myself and two other ladies had not seen it. The book evidently had been written back in November 2010 and was so successful the movie came out in April of 2014. The movie had been out for ten years. Again, one of the women who had seen the movie expressed how inspiring and especially comforting it was to her. She had lost a baby in late stage pregnancy just like the minister's wife in the movie. Colton, the minister's four year old son, was introduced to his older sister by Jesus. When the minister's wife asked him what she looked like, Colton responded, "She had hair the color of yours." She then asked him, "What was her name?" Colton responded, "You guys didn't give her a name". Prior to Linda's contact, I would have been looking for reasons and explanations and would not have accepted this as a gift from God.

When the cemetery plots became available, I scheduled Linda's internment. The cemetery no longer does interments on the weekend. It had to be a weekday. I scheduled it for a Monday to allow loved ones to get there without missing work, school, etc. I wanted to shout to the world the gift God had bestowed on me by allowing Linda to show me in my physical world she was still my soulmate and with me. However, by now I knew you had to pick and choose the right moment to share God's gift. If, in your desire to share, you barge ahead and force it on unsuspecting people that are just being sympathetic due to your loss, you will overpower them. They will do just like most of us have done all our lives, try to explain it away. It's difficult to accept what we have been taught through observation our entire lives is not possible on this earth. It's tough to believe something unbelievable if it doesn't happen to you personally.

I did get the opportunity to share our gift before I returned for the interment. It was a Saturday. I was leaving the next day to drive to Tennessee for the internment on Monday. I decided to get a hair trim. It was borderline whether to get it cut, really just a trim. I walked into my neighborhood, Great Clips. It was crowded and the beautician that normally cut my hair was busy. I almost turned around and walked out, after all I didn't really need a haircut. One young girl in the back section of the shop was headed my way. The last time I let a young beautician cut my hair, it hadn't gone well. I decided, I'll give her a chance. As we walked back to her station and I took a seat in her chair, I noticed a small tear roll down her cheek. She was softly crying.

Before Linda's passing and God's gift, I would not have invaded the girl's privacy and not revealed I was aware of her despair. As I sat down I asked her if she was okay. She began to explain that this was the first anniversary of her closest girlfriend's death. One year ago her friend had called her to go out. She had just gotten home from work and was tired. She had declined the invitation. Her friend went out alone. She had too much to drink and accidentally entered the highway traveling in the wrong direction and was killed. She had hit a truck head on. I sat there for a moment and thought about what I should say. I said, "You'll see her again". I then told her why I was getting a haircut and where I was going. I shared God's gift to Linda and me with her. By this time, we were both crying in a beauty shop full of customers and we didn't care. After she finished my trim and walked up front and I paid my bill, she looked at me and said, "God sent me you today". I think he did. I didn't really need a haircut!

The internment went well with many additional friends and family attending that were not able or aware of her January 2nd service. Our first born, Trey shared wonderful memories and insights into Linda's mothering and caring during his childhood. It was a casual affair. It was a beautiful day. We stood under a large canopy and went around the group and anyone who wanted to share was encouraged. The cemetery had Linda's casket displayed under the canopy and I had brought the oil painting of Linda that was displayed at her memorial service in January. Linda's presence was felt but not emanating from the casket. Her presence was all around. I think Linda enjoyed and approved the ceremony. A few really stood out. Her first cousin, Paula, really stood out. She is five or six years younger than Linda and me. She recounted how she and her friend Ann would hide upstairs and secretly look out the window and watch Linda and me when I brought Linda home after a date. I had to have Linda home by a certain time, especially on school nights. Our habit was to beat the timeline and be sitting in front of her house in the driveway to meet her parents wishes. We would then sit, talk and do what young people that care about each other do, smooch or neck. We were not aware anyone was watching us. If I overstayed my time in Linda's driveway, one of her parents would appear at the window or let us know it was time to come in the house. Only on one occasion did her father come out onto the front porch and proclaim, "Don't you think it's about time you went home young man"? I guess we had missed their subtle signal. Overall, the interment was a joyous experience but it was also very difficult. I knew Linda's spirit and soul was not in that casket, she was with us, but her body was there. It was a new section of the cemetery. It was the only broken ground in that area. It stood alone with a small bouquet laying on the fresh earth... the reality of our physical world on display at its worst.

After the interment, I stayed over in Tennessee and went shopping for a monument for Linda and me. Just the thought of that process would have been extremely difficult just a few months before. As everything in life, we were going to share a headstone. I was surprised at how emotionally removed I was from the process. At this juncture, I was well aware that this headstone would only mark the spot of our human remains. It would not represent where Linda and I were. I wasn't doing this for us, I was doing this for those not yet passed over. A long established tradition to give the living a place to pay their respects is now how I view this. A process that I had envisioned as morbid and totally distasteful was little more than fulfilling our obligation to our living loved ones and their descendants. It did answer something that had puzzled me for many years. Linda's best friend from high school married a mortician. He became a man I admired very much. He was simply a great person and turned out to be one of my best friends. I quickly realized he had something special about him. He was one that lived with God's grace. He was fun loving and lived life to its fullest yet he was a mortician. How could he do it? How was he able to fulfill his duties as a mortician? I now saw the answer to my question. He was able to perform the duties of a mortician because he had the knowledge of knowing these bodies he prepared for burial were just that, they contained no souls. He was simply assisting and consoling those loved ones left behind to grieve. He later changed his profession and became a successful manager at a major consumer products company.

The cemetery gave me three local monument companies. I went to their top recommendation first. It was only a few miles from the cemetery. It was a family business operated by a married couple. The husband had a separate office. The wife was the receptionist and sales person. She had a nice office and they had a couple of dogs they took to work with them. I had my dog, Billy, with me. I took him in with me and the owners welcomed Billy and the other dogs paid him little attention. I sat down with the wife to discuss my reason for being there and my overall situation. In the conversation, I commented that in her business she must hear a great deal about passed loved ones returning and visiting those left on earth. She said no never, tell me. My father just lost his wife and is having a tough time. I assumed it was a second marriage for her father or she would have said mom. I briefly told her about Linda's assistance in writing her eulogy and additional guidance in writing a letter to our grandchildren to help them in their search for salvation. I said I had extra copies of the letter to our grandchildren and would love to share it with her. We had a wonderful meeting and she told me of something that happened with her grandfather that was obviously one of God's gifts. I gathered her information and pricing and informed her I was going to shop around and would get back to her.

I visited the other two recommendations and made the same conclusion the cemetery had made. The first monument company was head and shoulders above the other two. When I walked back into the first monument company I visited, she greeted me affectionately. She seemed so glad I came back. I thought she was referring to the fact that she had made a sale. She wasn't. She told me she had shared our letter to our grandchildren with her father. She had faxed him a copy. He had sent her a long text. She allowed me to read it. He started out with, "Tell the man with the little dog how inspirational our letter was to him". He was convinced he too will be with his wife again. It was quite long for a text but it was simply telling us how he appreciated us sharing our gift with him. Linda and God were affecting more and more lives with His gift. I felt good about myself for the small part I had played in giving this stranger some peace dealing with his grief. I was aware God's grace had changed me. I was much bolder in my support of God and taking advantage of the opportunities presented to me. We were making a difference.

I then sat down with the wife and began to talk about the monument. She and her husband had done a computer print out of what the monument would look like. Unknown to me, she had put an inscription on the back of the monument. I had told her our last words to each other. On the back she had put, "Can I have all your Kisses" and underneath she had put, "Sure".

I came to realize that my goal in life had been primarily to make Linda's life as good as possible, to protect and make sure no harm came to her. I owed her everything. She made my life "Heaven on earth". It had come as a huge awakening that I had very little to say in the matter. It was all under God's control. At first I felt I had failed her. Why didn't I do this or why didn't I do that. I could have saved her. I was remiss. I didn't realize it was going to end so soon. I remembered something Glen had said to me many years ago. Glen and Susie were visiting. Something came up, I don't remember what. Linda informed me she had already taken care of something and it was handled. It's unimportant what it was but that without my input, she had handled it. Shortly after, Linda and Susie left the room to go do something. I looked at Glen and remarked, "When did I lose control"? Glen answered, "Dad, you never had control." He was joking and correct at the time, I was never in control when Linda was physically with me because by this time I was aware of the wiser between us. I now realize I was never in control in determining when Linda's life would end. It is God's will. She was the most precious thing in my life. I adore everything about her and always will. I wanted to save her, but I feel just the opposite has happened. When I think about the depth of my love for Linda, I can't love or appreciate her enough to ever repay her for spending her magnificent life with a wretch like me. Just the name "Linda Donaldson" exalts me. Always has since I first met her. My dream girl. My dream human being. How can I repay her for her love of me? I can't. Now she has even come back to save my soul.

Prior to starting this book, I was looking for something to occupy the long days without her physically with me. I no longer needed to take care of her. I no longer needed to fix her meals, wash her clothes. Nothing! Our little dog was missing her as well. He would run to the door when someone showed up and other actions indicated he was looking for her. He stuck to me like glue. I decided I would get him a friend to ease his loneliness. I contacted the breeder where we had purchased Billy, and he had the perfect little girl dog. I decided to drive the sixty five miles to his farm to look the dog over. My first cousin was crazy about our little dog and told me if I ever go back to his farm and he has a dog like Billy, he wants it. When I got there he had a full sister to Billy with the same mother and father. The breeder had named her Daisy. She was only twelve weeks old, Billy was now about three years old. She is beautiful and sweet. I took a picture and texted it to him. He liked her and told me he wanted her. I bought Daisy and the puppy I had gone to see, Rosey, and headed home with my three dogs. On the way home, my cousin called and informed me he just can't do it. He had adopted a rescued two year old female dog that had been abused. He just couldn't take her back to the pound and he couldn't handle two dogs. I totally understood and applauded his loyalty. However, I now had three dogs, Billy, Rosey and Daisy. When I got home a neighbor informed me the HOA only allows for two dogs. I now had what I called my pack. One of my close neighbors had just lost one of her small dogs and her remaining dog was very lonely. She had been asking me to bring Billy over so they could play. She would sometimes come by and take Billy with her on their walks. I took the two new dogs to her and she fell for Rosey. She said she wanted her but she couldn't take her right away as they had just placed her sister in a nursing home some forty miles away and she would be occupied the next few weeks getting her settled and situated. I told her certainly but my problem with three dogs was settled. Perhaps a month went by when she came to me and informed me she must back out of taking Rosey because her sister is not doing well. By this time these two puppies are inseparable. They were both taken away from their mothers and bonded immediately. I can't separate them. By this time I am attached to both of them. When I am missing Linda and lonely, I can put those puppies on the couch with me and they are all over me. I wish I had gotten them when Linda was physically with me.

During my search to find a good home for one of my new puppies. I was discussing my problem with my sister Barbara and her husband, Layfield. Let me introduce you to Layfield. He is a great guy. A self made man that has been very successful with his own business. He had a special unspoken relationship with our dad and you could see the admiration and love between them. Layfield and I have wonderful memories of adventures we went on as young adults. We laugh about it today because he always came out on the short end of the stick in our adventures. Back to the point. I was explaining my predicament to them. I was aware Layfield did not want the responsibility of a new puppy. I was kidding him and telling him all the love and advantages a puppy brings you. He was adamant about not wanting a dog. Several weeks later I texted a video of the puppies playing and as usual I was talking baby talk to them. Barbara was sharing the video with him and Layfield, being a man of few words, remarked, "Howard is going to keep all those damn dogs". A classic Layfield remark, direct and to the point, and as usual, correct.

For those family members that witnessed God's gift while we were writing her eulogy and those family members that really know us, it's easy to believe. For those that don't know us, they immediately start to look for possible worldly explanations. Linda continues to come to me. When I started this book she set me straight again. I was writing and decided I would add a statement that would make me look a little purer or godly. It wasn't technically true. As I began to type I started the statement. I typed, we were both, the computer would not allow me to type any further. It would just make a bonk noise when I tried to type. My computer expert, my granddaughter, was upstairs and I called up to her for help. She came down and I showed her what the computer was doing. She took over the keyboard and attempted to get it working. She was having no success.

She finally said, "What are you trying to type". I was forced to reconsider what it was I was about to write. Reluctantly, I told her it was not a true statement. I knew and I am certain now Linda knew, it was not true. Linda stopped me from putting a needless lie into something we were attempting to save souls and bring souls to Jesus Christ and salvation. It would have ruined everything we were trying to convey. I had not written the statement, just thinking about what I was going to write and Linda had stopped me. I told my granddaughter the statement didn't need to be included and told her I would not include it. The computer allowed me to continue with no further input from either one of us.

I continue to have questions. Why are there no books in the Bible written by women, with perhaps the exception of Priscilla in the book of Hebrews? Linda was the most godly human being I've ever known. She not only talked the talk, she walked the walk as they say. She did unto others as she would have them do unto her. Linda honored God and Jesus Christ by the way she lived her life. Linda, through the grace of God and Jesus Christ, has removed my doubts. She continues to assist me and give me the courage to serve our Father by doing His will. We are writing this, whatever it is, together. If I get stuck on what to write, she comes to my aid. I'm not getting the little flags anymore but she is letting me know she agrees with what we are attempting to communicate. I guess I will have to wait to get all my answers. I look forward to her next suggestions. I guess I will continue to add new input from Linda as it occurs while completing this document.

FULFILLING GOD'S PLAN

I am aware of what God wants me to do for the remainder of my life here on earth. He wants me to, and I long to, serve him. I want to witness by how I live my life and treat my fellow man and reflect God's love for us. I want to bring as many souls as possible to Jesus Christ and the Holy Spirit. This is a result of God's gift of allowing Linda to contact me after she passed. Her contact and guidance with God's grace has brought a wretch like me to salvation. I have gone from somewhat dreading Sunday because

I had to go to church. When I went to church I felt better about myself but I'm not sure I was closer to God, because I had never opened my heart and soul to the Holy Spirit. Thanks to Linda and the grace of God, Jesus Christ and the Holy Spirit, now Sunday is by far my favorite day of the week. I can't wait to get to church with my brothers and sisters and honor God. My goal is to honor my soulmate with the way I live my life and make her proud. I want to keep listening to her and the Lord's guidance.

I am embarrassed in church. As I feel the Holy Spirit and God's love, I am overpowered with emotion. I begin to cry during the service. I think I am crying from joy and gratitude not from grief. Why am I embarrassed? I'm aware that those people sitting directly behind me can't hear me but can see my back shaking as I try to conceal my crying. I see other worshipers extending their arms up in the air with them open wide, why am I reluctant to do so? I am so thankful for the blessings I have received. How can I ever repay my wonderful blessings? When I consider the blessings it removes all doubts about the almighty. He created the heavens and earth. He created man in his image. This means he has created everything Linda and I have ever known in life. Every person we have ever met, God has created. Even those people we have walked by on the sidewalk. He created all our forefathers, right back to Adam and Eve. He created everyone we have come to love in our life. He created the love of my life and made it possible for our two souls to meet. Why am I embarrassed to openly show my love for Jesus? I hope it is that I don't want people who are sitting around me to think I am crying from grief or loss. I know I have work to do in this area.

I do see a major change in myself. I am Irish and I have an Irish temper. It has gotten me in many awkward situations in my life. I have attempted to keep it in check for as long as I can remember. It was extremely rare to ever see the temper emotion from Linda. I honestly can only think of one time and it was because of me. It was innocent on my part playing my little put down game but it hurt her feelings and I saw a rare side of her. But this thinking I was being cute or funny and in a kidding way putting someone down is a terrible habit to get into. I don't think I started it, I hope not, but it has become a habit throughout our extended family. At family gatherings, this type of friendly banter was always present. Most of the time it was our way of cutting up and playing with one another. Occasionally, someone would go too far and hurt someone's feelings. I think we need to come up with a new way of showing our affection and love for each other rather than attempting to one up them. I have made a concerted effort not to engage in this game.

I don't recall Linda doing this to anyone. Linda liked to play but it was done with obvious affection. An example of this, we created several gardens around our lawn and home after retirement. I became interested in garden plants and flowers. One day I had to run an errand without Linda and stopped by the nursery on my way home. When I pulled into the driveway, Linda was working in one of our larger gardens bordered by the driveway. I parked alongside the garden and began to unload rose bushes I had just purchased. Linda looked at me and in a sweet voice said, "Did my little fella buy himself some flowers"? I didn't take it as a putdown, I took it as affection. I was her little fella and I loved being Linda's little fella. She gave me a rose bush and card on father's day and signed it to my little fella. One of our grandchildren overheard us talking about it and the name stuck, her little fella. I hope to be Linda's little fella forever.

As I have mentioned earlier, since Linda's passing, I have been grabbing at straws to ease the grief and pain from Linda's physical absence. I went back to where we found our little dog, Billy, and purchased two additional puppies. They have proved to be difficult to house train so I am allowing them to play in the attached garage several hours a day. One day I didn't back out the car before opening the door and letting them into the garage. Later in the day, I put the puppies back into the laundry room as I was leaving to go to the grocery store. I looked around the garage to see if the puppies had relieved themselves in the garage. I didn't see anything and opened the car door to enter the car. My front foot stepped slightly under the car and I felt something squishy. I knew immediately, I had stepped in dog poop. I was in the garage and I retrieved my little lawn trowel we used to plant flowers and pot plants. The bulk of the poop I picked up with a poopy bag and discarded in the garbage can. The small amount I scraped off my shoe, rather than throw it out in the lawn, I walked through the neighbors lawn to the woods beside our condos. I live in a community of fourplex condos. These woods are made up of large bushes of honeysuckle and small native trees. I think all together there are seventeen acres of vacant land but it adjoins several small farms on the other side. It is virtually a wildlife sanctuary next to our condos. We hear coyotes yelping at night and five deer came out of the area one day I was walking Billy. Many song birds nest in the area. As I turned from throwing the small scrapings from my shoe back under the honeysuckle, my neighbor was standing on his patio which overlooks the woods. He said, "Did I just see you throw dog shit into the woods?" I told him I did because I had just stepped in it in my garage. He began to berate me. He said things like you would think you would have more respect for your neighbors than to do that. I tried to explain I always have respect for my neighbors. I said, "You're kidding aren't you". I always pickup my dog's poop. I even pickup other dogs poop that their owners don't pickup. He would not relent. This went on for several statements and I could see the anger on his face.

I let my Irish anger get the best of me and said his name, and then said "F —You". He wanted to keep talking and even said, "Let's finish this". I told him as far as I'm concerned it is finished. I don't want to live next door to someone with this much destain for me and walked away. That little piece of dog poop wasn't going to pollute the area and is nothing considering the amount of poop being distributed in those words daily by the wildlife that call it home.

I walked into my house and walked right into a large picture of Linda hanging on our dining room wall. It hit me like a ton of bricks. Is that a Godly way to treat your neighbor? She let me know she agreed, he was out of line but you haven't walked in his shoes. You don't know what he is going through. I feel Linda knew what he was going through. I turned right around and went back out the door and walked to my neighbors house. He was no longer on his patio. I rang his front door bell. When he came to the door I told him I was sorry for saying "F—You". He immediately began to apologize saying he was way over the top, etc. He explained how he had chosen his condo because it was next to the woods and secluded. He had stopped people that didn't even live in the neighborhood from dumping things back there. He brought up something about age and it turns out we are the same age and both are Irish. After the conversation, he reached out his hand to shake and I put my arms around him and hugged him. I would have never made that jester before Linda and the Lord took hold of me. I felt for him. I fear he is going through what Linda and I have just gone through and he is angry at the world. We all have to go through it.

I see the changes taking hold. Just this past Sunday, I went to brunch after the early service at church with three family members. The bantering started up between the family. I didn't join in. I normally would have. Two of the family members were piling on the third person. Nothing really bad but pointing out shortcomings that had an element of truth. It was clear, the one they were ganging up on was not enjoying it at all. Their barbs had enough truth to hurt. I looked at the ones throwing the barbs and commented something about, we just came from church. The two ganging up smiled and stopped. It switched to a great family time together that everyone will remember fondly. I know it is a little thing and not a big deal. But that family member they were ganging up on appreciated my intervention, I could see it in her eyes. I felt Jesus was at work through me and it felt good.

I have observed the changes in most family members that knew Linda. Salvation and studying the scriptures has become the center of our lives. It seems Jesus is directing every sermon to us. This past week's sermon pointed out, sometimes you have to reach rock bottom before you will open your heart and soul to the Lord. Hitting rock bottom for me was losing Linda. I was at the bottom of bottom. The center of my world was taken away. The one I loved above any other living thing and the person that loved me more than anyone has, was gone from my physical life. Everyone that really knew Linda was aware she had no malice in her heart. She wanted everyone to be happy and witnessed God's teachings through the way she lived her life and treated those she touched. Jesus lived within her. This is my goal. To witness by the way I live my life and allow Jesus to work through me. To give me the wisdom and skills to reach fellow souls with his promise.

I had reached rock bottom and felt I had nothing to live for. God has shown me through Jesus Christ and the Holy Spirit, I have a tremendous amount to live for. Every soul is special and needs God's mercy. I have wonderful people all around me. I observe everyday what my kids are attempting to do for me to lessen my grief. I see Linda's influence in their caring. I want all God's children with us in heaven. We all have a lot to do. It is easy to observe my son and his wife, they only live four miles away from me. I watch them put aside their health issues and family problems to include me in their lives to lessen my loss. I see so much of Linda in him. God's goal I feel is to see this love for all God's children in all of us.

This past week's church service made me aware of something I hadn't even considered. We studied the book of Acts 9 and the conversion of Saul from the vicious persecutor of the Lord's disciples to Jesus's chosen instrument to proclaim his name to the world. Jesus called on Ananias as the one to lay his hands on Saul and let the Lord work through him to heal his sight and fill him with the Holy Spirit. The minister pointed out that Ananias does not appear anywhere else in the bible. Saul goes on to later become the apostle Paul and converts many followers to Jesus Christ. The minister then made the analysis of who converted the reverend Billy Graham to the Lord and Jesus Christ. Who was his "Ananias"? Reverend Billy Graham, a man who was responsible for introducing millions of souls to the Lord and salvation, we don't even know the name of his Ananias.

The minister then asked the congregation who was their Saul in their circle of family and friends. We all have them, they may not be terrorists and murderers like Saul but they do need someone to introduce them to the Lord. Their souls are worth saving. Linda and I plan to give our "Saul's" this book and tell them that we love them.

HEAVEN AND HOPE

Thanks to God's grace by allowing Linda to reach me through our physical world I have proof your soul does not perish when our physical body passes. This one act removed all doubt that we are created in our maker's image and our spirit is not bound by this physical world. This I now know.

I don't have many answers and there is much more I don't know than I do know, but the Bible says all will be revealed to us and I do believe that it will. I know neither Linda nor I knew how to collaborate while writing a document prior to her passing. I still didn't know how and she had to keep making parts or all of the document disappear so I would seek help from someone that could explain what was happening. someone that was more literate with computers and software to recognize that she was helping me write her eulogy. She also knew I wasn't going back and proofreading the document and fixing the other little flags she didn't agree with and had to call on another family member to tell me what she was conveying to them. I am equally convinced she is still communicating with me. She is guiding me and suggesting what needs to be done here on earth before I join her. She has done it while attempting to write this book. While writing this book, I was thinking about including a statement that really didn't need to be included. The computer quit working and would just make a sound and would not operate. I hadn't written it, only thinking about it. When I decided not to type that thought because it was not true, she released the computer. Linda kept me from writing an untruth and damaging the book, amazing, and only with the grace of God!

Through this process, I have come to some conclusions that I feel are true. God loves us. God is love. Love is the most powerful and lasting emotion of all our emotions, and God gave us that. The only soul that is with you from your very first thought until your last is your soul and the Lord. The Lord is always with you.

If you're lucky enough to meet your soulmate as I was, you love that soul above your own. You feel incomplete without them. They are what makes you. They are so special, that them loving you makes you special. Without them you are lost. When Linda passed, I was lost. Every second without her was hell, total despair and eternal loneliness, nothing else mattered. Then once again, Jesus graced us with his love. The Lord has given Linda and me the gift of letting her show me His love, by proving to me not only does your soul live on but that she is with Him. She was able to teach me that all of our lives are just a moment in time and a necessary step to bigger and greater things. Linda is with me, not in the physical sense but with her spirit and soul she is with me at all times. Together, we can still do anything and perhaps more than we could when we were physically together. God does not make unfulfilled promises. If you believe God gave his only

Son for our sins so that we would have everlasting life in heaven and accept him as your Savior and allow the Holy Spirit into your soul, you will have everlasting life in heaven.

This brings us to the question, what is Heaven like? We all know what we hope heaven would be like. Happiness, satisfaction, blissful, lacking nothing. So wonderful we can't even imagine how wonderful Heaven is, full of love and kindness. Heaven would be void of all the evil emotions like greed, envy, hate and the list goes on and on. Heaven to me would contain everyone I love, especially the love of my life. I think God's gifts to us allow us little bits and pieces of heaven if we will accept them for the gifts they are. Since Linda and I personally received one of these gifts, we know anything is possible under God. I believe the four year old little boy in Nebraska, Colton, portrayed in the movie, "Heaven is for real", did go to heaven. I do believe the things he told his mother and father, he actually experienced in heaven. According to Colton, there is no time in heaven, nobody wears glasses, nobody is old, lots of animals, heaven is just like here only prettier, etc. Linda has given vague indications. When I pass a restaurant that she likes I wish she were here to enjoy it again, she lets me know that she is doing fine. Linda basically lets me know it's wonderful where she is. She tells me I shouldn't feel sorry for her, suggesting I have not seen anything yet. I know this is true. Linda refused to lie while physically with me and is not lying to me now. I don't know where heaven is. Where it is isn't important, just that there is heaven and it's wonderful.

There is evil in the world and Satan is constantly tempting us. We have all given into these temptations. I am finding with the Holy Spirit in my soul, these temptations are greatly reduced and easier to control. I have trouble explaining or understanding how God allows some things to happen, how some things that mankind does or has done in history is allowed to happen.

When I think of the genocide that has occurred throughout history I don't know the answer. When you see small children fighting cancer that don't get the same opportunities that God has afforded you and your loved ones, it doesn't seem fair. What is the purpose of this suffering? These things have no answer with our limited knowledge. We will know when all is revealed to us.

I watched Linda accept what life dealt her with grace. My darling girl is the wisest and most humble soul I know along with my grandmother. Linda is blessed by God.

She was born into a loving and Christian family. She is beautiful and wise. She is athletic with natural abilities, especially where balance is concerned. Linda has more to lose than most. She has it all. I might be a little prejudiced where Linda is concerned. She took life's challenges head on and took setbacks in stride and made the most of them. Other than some false and unfounded accusations made against her from a close family member, she handled every challenge. She wisely handled this problem after she passed.

As you know, she has communicated with me on many occasions since then. Exposing these communications is the purpose for this book. Because of these revelations, I don't think death is as bad as I did before Linda with God's grace came back to save a wretch like me. I used to think possibly death was the end and going on blind faith and hoping there was heaven. Now I feel death it's only the beginning. Our time on earth is a flash in time as compared to eternity. I do believe God gives us gifts to make it easier for us to accept his truths.

I have many questions and my darling girl has directed me back to church and the Bible for answers. In order to believe one needs answers. Linda is telling me look to the Bible. There have been a few people that I have known, I knew were children of God. Linda was first on that list. Another was my grandmother on my mother's side. Two male friends or neighbors that stand out I have known or come in contact with over the years wear God's grace everyday. One was a neighbor back in my young adulthood that stood in my garage and confidently professed that the scriptures and salvation is not about what you can't do but the possibilities of what you can do. I heard what he said but didn't really understand the depth of his statement at the time. He was my neighbor across the street from us with a wife and young kids. Friendly with a great sense of humor but had a different aura about him. It was evident in everything he said and did, he was at peace with himself and confident about his belief. I wished I could have been that secure in my belief. The other gentleman that stood out in my life was the husband of one of Linda's best friends throughout school. Linda's friend had gone through a rough first marriage that had ended in divorce. Her friend went to work as a receptionist at a local funeral home. She met her second husband there as he was a mortician. What an outstanding man he was. So full of life. Lived life to the fullest but always quietly paid homage to the Lord. He too had that special aura about him, humble and wise. We vacationed with them and another couple for over twenty five years. He would quietly and without any fanfare go outside and find a place to pray and read the Bible. He passed away a few years ago and we traveled to his funeral in Charlotte. I was amazed at the praise this man received at his memorial service. One after another stood up and confessed, he was my best friend and how he had changed their life. The other couple we vacationed with came to the Lord during this period of time and I feel he was a major influence on them. His wife recently told me she has been amazed by the vast number and diversity of people that felt the need to express their appreciation toward this disciple of God and the positive impact he has had on their lives. You can add me to that list.

As I stated earlier, Linda and I let this world's old age slip up on us. We weren't kids and certainly time had diminished our physical abilities, but we weren't old. Linda's little hands were the same little hands I had held all my life. I adored everything about her. She is still gorgeous to me. We made plans like this love affair was going to last forever. She still has that sweet precious spirit I fell head over heels for when I was a teenager. It was clear to see the effect age and life were having on both of us. The obvious wrinkles, loss of hair color, muscle tone and mental capacity. I feel the rheumatoid medication and resulting TIA's, hastened the mental decline for Linda. I did not want to accept Linda's little losses as they appeared. I tried to ignore them thinking they would fix themselves or maybe if I tried harder, I could fix it. In an instant, it was all over. Total despair. Like falling in an endless abyss. I couldn't fix it. I fell short. Way short. Oh my God, life is over. My heaven with Linda is gone.

Salvation! God loves all his children and is inviting us to join him in heaven. God with his mercy and grace allowed Linda to show me that your soul survives. God loves me. God, through his grace, has shown me he loves me as deep or deeper than I can love. He has given me opportunities all my life to fully accept his grace and I have refused. I would try very hard thinking, I'm a good guy, I'll stack up a large number of accomplishments God will approve of and he will forgive my shortcomings. He has shown me through the one I treasure most on this earth, Linda, it doesn't work that way.

We can't save ourselves or our loved ones by being a good guy or living a life where the good deeds outweigh the bad. We can't save ourselves through religion and just studying the Bible and living a christian life. God went to great lengths to save my soul. He gave me everything, storybook childhood complete with wonderful parents and siblings, wonderful extended family.

Allowed me to meet my soulmate who directed my life and allowed me to observe how a child of God lives their life and attempted to keep me in church. Everything God had afforded me wasn't enough to persuade me to accept God's grace and mercy. I continued to live this physical life by the rules it imposes on us to be successful and to covet worldly things. God took away the one thing that would totally get my attention and bring me to my knees, loss of my soulmate.

Her physical death took me to the very bottom. From this black darkness, God, through Linda, has shown me the light and everlasting life. Jesus gave his life so Linda and I will have an everlasting life together. We will be with all God's children in heaven forever. The knowledge we gain when passing over can't be verbalized. Linda had been compromised on earth by her illness and life. When God's grace allowed Linda to return to me, she was restored completely. She had knowledge she didn't have while living. We can only imagine. Your spirit has an energy that can't be extinguished. Just like Linda painted my heart with her love she is soothing my soul with her love and knowledge after her passing. She and God have conveyed my purpose on earth. I long to serve him. In the meantime, I miss Linda's physical presence and I yearn to be with her. I do have the comfort of sixty three years of wonderful memories with the love of my life and the knowledge that she is with me spiritually until God has me pass over.

I had thought about what would happen when we were parted by death. I thought about years ago when I had my heart attack and resulting double bypass surgery. I was 59 years old riding with a group of young men my son's age. We were down in Kentucky riding motorcycles on twisty country roads far from any medical center. It took 2 1/2 hours for the ambulance to find me and get me to a small clinic in Maysville, Kentucky, a small

Ohio river town in Kentucky and home of singer Rosemary Clooney and her nephew George Clooney. I was airlifted to a major hospital in Cincinnati. The heart attack had lasted until mid flight flying to Cincinnati. As soon as I could breath, the paramedic said, "It's stopped hasn't it". It had. As I flew onto the helicopter pad on the hospital, I realized I was floating over the waiting room inside the hospital. I was well above the hospital waiting room and it was fairly crowded. I spotted Linda among the visitors gathered in the waiting room. I couldn't see her face but I would recognize that pretty little head anywhere. Even looking down on it. I remember conveying to her I was sorry for having the heart attack and putting her through this stress. It was an experience like the one Colton experienced in the movie, "Heaven is for Real".

Several days later, while I was recovering from the surgery, a nurse was interviewing Linda and me. We had explained what had occurred. She looked at me and said, "It wasn't your time. That's the only explanation". She was referring to the length of time the attack had lasted and the length of time before I received medical attention. I have thought about that statement a great deal over the 21 years since that attack. I knew our relationship was special. We were simply meant to be together. I secretly thought about the prospect, if one of us passes before the other, will the one that passes over return to let the surviving spouse know everythings okay. Obviously, I was thinking it would be me passing first due to the heart issue.

I now wonder if it had been me, would God have shown me the grace to allow me to come back to Linda? I think he would have because God is a merciful God. God has lit a fire in my soul to make my soulmate proud of what we can do together on this earth before we are together in heaven.

The review of this manuscript has resulted in some truly thought provoking conclusions and reveals. God created Heaven and Earth. As I've already stated, life without Linda was hell. The deepest abyss one can imagine. Through this process, it has become clear that one can't choose and pick a ranking order for those loved ones. You either love them or you don't. You love each individual uniquely. There is a special place in your heart for each and everyone of those you love. Heaven must include Linda and therefore all your loved ones or it wouldn't be heaven. The almighty wouldn't provide us with an almost heaven. Room and space would never be a problem. God loves all his children and wants us all with Him in Heaven. God is love.

Another discovery of this process is that you love those the deepest that love us the deepest. I knew Linda put me first on her list and her on mine. We lived our lives for each other. We knew each other's frailties and loved them more. God has put us all first. How can you deny his love? The Lord has given us everything we have. The Lord created Heaven and Earth and everything in it, including everyone and everything we cherish. He gave his only Son for our sins.

I think about all the beings I have loved in my life. As I am writing this, it's 3:32 AM in the morning. I have a driving desire to complete this testament, accounting of events, or whatever this document is and allow the Lord to do with it what He will. I'm back at the stool at the bar in the kitchen, at my feet is our little dog, Billy. I love him and I can see the trust and love in his eyes. I can feel his love for me when he snuggles up to me. He is here with me on the cold floor because he would rather be close to me on the cold floor than be in a warm soft bed. This kind of love and devotion is special. It makes me think of my dog while growing up, Taffy. She was a mixed breed spaniel, mostly cocker. She was my closest buddy growing up. She went virtually everywhere I went. She was a protector of everything mine, especially my bicycle. When I went into the local store and parked my bike outside, she wouldn't allow anyone close to it. I saw and felt the love in her eyes. I see it in Billy's eyes. Billy has been so comforting to me dealing with the physical loss of Linda. I saw this love in the eyes of a pet duck I acquired as a kid. I purchased this baby duck from a local feed store. It was in the spring and somewhat cold outside. My parents would not allow me to have a pet duck, we lived in a subdivision. The lot directly behind us was vacant with tall wild grasses. My mother had a large white porcelain bucket. I hid my duck, Chipper, in this bucket behind our house with a heavy mesh wire over the top when I didn't have him with me. I was in the sixth grade. I took Chipper everywhere I could. I even snuck him into the Saturday matinee theater in my jacket pocket. Everywhere I went, Taffy, Chipper and I were together. I hadn't had Chipper for a couple of weeks or perhaps a month when I was playing in the next door neighbor's backyard. I had Chipper out in his bucket with food and water as I was playing with my childhood friend Robby. Long story but stupidly, I managed to fall off the neighbor's swing set, head first. The result was, I broke both arms just above the wrist. I don't remember much about the hospital but I had broken both bones in my left arm and it was a compound fracture. When I came to after the surgery, my mother wanted to know what I was murmuring about Chipper. I needed to take care of Chipper. I was forced to confess to purchasing a baby duck and hiding him out in a vacant field behind our house, in order to save his life. He would die of starvation or dehydration unless someone rescued him. My parents were so thankful that I was okay and would recover from my injuries, they allowed me to keep Chipper. Chipper grew up to be a beautiful big white duck. He slept in the garage with my dog, Taffy. Chipper in his large bushel basket and Taffy in her bed next to Chipper. When we traveled throughout the neighborhood visiting neighbors it was a procession. Me or Taffy in the lead with Chipper quacking or chirping along behind us. I think the neighbors enjoyed having Chipper in their lives. It's not everyday you see this kind of friendship and love between animals. Nothing bothered Chipper when Taffy was around. I saw this love in both their eyes. They loved each other and I loved them both. When Chipper was approximately two years old, my parents took me to a local park that contained a large lake and several resident white domestic ducks. We took Chipper to visit. The first place we took him, he followed us back to the car and we took him home. A few weeks later we took him to a lake that had a large number of domestic white ducks like himself. He loved it. He immediately blended in. I knew it was the best place for him. My parents took me back several weeks in a row. The first few weeks, Chipper came immediately to me. Then slowly he would come to me and immediately go back to his friends. Chipper had found home.

I have often wondered if there are animals in heaven. I believe there will be. All our loved ones will be in heaven. It's now 4:31 AM and Billy is still laying on the cold floor at my feet. Yes, I think Billy, Taffy, Chipper, Lucy and Scooter (our cats) will be in heaven. I wouldn't be heaven without them all.

God continues to work his miracles through Linda and now me. God has worked miracles on me. He has fundamentally changed me forever. With Jesus Christ dwelling within, I am saved and free from the rules of this physical world. Linda's immediate family knows how she lived her life and now see the power of the Lord after she passed. Those family members close to Linda and her passing have had their faith restored and enforced. They are following the Lord's teaching and attending church services to be with other children of God. More importantly, they are trying to witness God's love through how they conduct their lives.

This body God has bestowed us does perish. It happens to all God's children. Everyone on earth must go through the passing on or demise of the human body. When I look back at my life with Linda it seems like yesterday we were just starting out. Where did it go? Now it seems, time simply flew by. It flies by for all of us. Thanks to God's grace and mercy, we won't need to worry about time in heaven. Until then, we have a great deal to do to bring all God's children with us.

EPILOGUE

What does Linda's contacting me after she passed over tell us? For the most skeptical, at least, it indicates your soul does not perish when your physical body expires. That the returning soul can interact with the living. That the departed soul is aware of what you are doing and can assist you and provide guidance to the living. That the returning soul has gained tremendous knowledge and abilities by passing over. That the departed soul can communicate in both directions with the living. In my case, Linda could read my mind and was aware of what I was about to do and stopped me. That her soul has been made whole and free of any ailments. Linda is on top of everything and guiding the two of us through life and prioritizing what needs to be done.

Again, for the most skeptic, you can't see her, you can't touch her, you can't smell or hear her. You have a lot less than you had before she passed. That is true for now. But you have a tremendous amount more than you thought you had immediately after her passing. At the very least you know her soul is prospering. She is communicating with you mentally and you are consoled by her caring and desire to help. You can feel her presence with you and she is communicating that where she is is amazing. She is staying with you. Not everyday, but often I wake with the warmth only Linda can provide me. I know she has been with me. When I wake I look around for her because her presence is so strong. It has been six months, and we are still working together. That is quite a lot. You can go on doing what you need to do in this world until God brings you to her. At the very least, we will be with our loved ones spiritually. Death of your physical body is not the final act. I feel I can communicate with her at any second. That's pretty wonderful.

What did I have before God showed his mercy and power and allowed Linda to return to me? I was in hell, total despair and loss. I could not have sustained my existence on earth without God's gift of allowing Linda to show her love for me by consoling me that all is not lost. The loss was just too painful to possibly continue without her assuring me she is well and good. Hallelujah, she has!

What is the maximum Linda's return and communications are telling us? That everything God promises is true. If you accept Jesus as your savior and allow the Holy Spirit into your soul, God's grace will reside within you and you will have everlasting life in heaven. Accepting God's grace into your soul doesn't cost you a thing. It doesn't restrict the meaningful activities in this life, it expands your ability to do great things with your life. It soothes your soul and provides you great joy.

When we came to the decision to write this accounting of what has transpired here on earth since Linda's passing over she has continued to give me guidance and understanding. During this process, we have consulted with a local publisher and sought direction from other novice authors. Our goal is to share our knowledge as much as possible. To do this, we decided to go with a local professional publisher rather than going the cheapest route to getting the book on bookshelves and on the internet. Making a profit is not our goal. Reaching as many souls as possible is the goal. If it does turn out to miraculously turn a profit, God will guide us where to best do good.

This professional publisher immediately gave us great advice. He informed us that we had more or less written the events as if we were having a conversation. He felt we should disclose more about how I felt when Linda made her presence known to me, more than just writing we jumped up and down with joy. He said we needed to review the entire book and talk in more detail about these emotions. Don't hold back when writing about what was going through your mind as it was happening. As we started to do this, I was almost immediately reminded about what Linda and God's grace was telling me. It wasn't just that your soul doesn't perish when your physical body does. It was much, much deeper. Linda wasn't just telling me she "is". She was telling me, she will always be an "is". She will never be a "was". God promises everlasting life. We are all "is's". Everyone you love, everyone you know, everyone you pass on the street is an "is". None of us are "was's". It was as if my mind lit up. Of course, Jesus gave his life for our sins so we could have everlasting life. Not so our soul could hang around and help out the living and then go away. God keeps His promises. Your soul lives forever, a concept we humans have difficulty understanding.

It is difficult to totally accept God's gifts, even for me, and Linda and I were given this gift while other members of our family participated. The everyday reality of not having Linda physically with me is powerful. I catch myself getting extremely lonely and sad that I can't reach out and hold her. I begin to feel sorry for myself that we can't be totally together. That is when she reminds me, "I'm still here. This is how it is for the time being. Suck it up, my little fellow, and get the job done and we will have eternity to be together."

I think all of us can recognize someone that walks with God's grace. My pastor put it into words for me. He said, someone that walks with God's grace within them has a certain aura about them. I hope the sharing of God's gift to Linda and me will help you to achieve this aura.

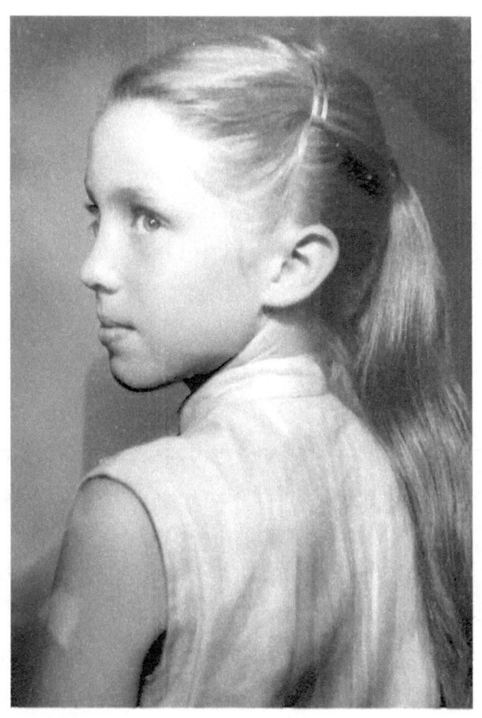

LINDA'S CELEBRATION

We are here today to celebrate Linda Donaldson Sullivan's physical life here on earth. Knowing Linda, she will continue to assist us in getting through our journey.

When I sat down and attempted to put my thoughts on paper it was almost impossible. We have all dreaded the thought of facing this day. As I struggled, it slowly emerged that I wasn't doing this alone. Linda and I were doing it together.

For those who know her, join me in thanking God for creating her and allowing her to touch our lives. As someone that was given the greatest gift of having her as my wife and soul mate for over 62 years, perhaps I know Linda better than anyone left here on earth.

Linda is fun-loving and loves life and displayed it throughout her life, right up until God said you're ready to come home. In my eyes she was born ready, but God had a mission for her and she made straight A's. Linda is beautiful, both physically and spiritually. Her physical beauty is what drew me to her. When I first saw her, she was on a football field marching up and down the field twirling a baton. She stood out. She was the cutest thing I'd ever seen, she had this long ponytail that went all the way down her back. Logic kicked in and I dismissed attempting to pursue her because she was way above my head, but I did learn her name, just in case, Linda Donaldson. Our first face to face meeting was a few blocks from this very chapel, the Dairy Gold on the corner of Brainerd and Moore road. In the spring of 1961, I pulled into the Dairy Gold to get lunch. Walking towards the front door, it took me directly by a red convertible full of six pretty girls. I realized it was too late to change my approach without being noticed. I felt a little intimidated, I was outnumbered and outgunned. Linda and her beautiful ponytail was sitting in the back seat far right corner, the side I was walking by. As I passed her I heard this pretty little voice say, "Hey". I turned around and said hey. She asked me if I could bring her some salt. I don't know exactly what I said. The request was so unusual it took me by surprise, but I tried to be cool and went inside and brought her a salt shaker off a table. I took it back to Linda and asked her if there was anything else she needed. We still have that salt shaker. Fate or God intervened a couple of more times before we actually dated for the first time.

When we began to date is when I quickly realized this is the girl I want to spend the rest of my life with. Unlike what she was,

SPECIAL, her personality and attitude was down to earth and humble. She doesn't think she is special. Linda is a caring and loving soul. She has always considered others before herself and this continues today as we meet. Linda has the most common sense of anyone I've ever known. Throughout our marriage, she was always right but she never flaunted this fact. She makes everyone around her better in virtually every way. Linda is a classy and stylish woman but does it very quietly.

Linda and I are connected at the hip. She is my everything. She is the love of my life, my best friend, my rock, my sounding board, my reason for getting up in the morning, incredible wife and mother to our children. In short, she is my soulmate. Heck, we even have the same email. After we had retired, we saw no need to maintain two separate emails. We still have our joint email.

Linda loved to go out to eat with family and friends, travel (driving vacations were her favorite), and antiquing. She often said, I don't understand depression. She always makes the most of her circumstances. She loves every facet of life. Linda even approached her chores and made them fun. Linda enjoyed laundry and she was a master at it. Our linens and towels were folded better than the finest hotels. Our socks and clothes were always folded perfectly in our draws. She took pride in performing these mundane tasks. I overheard Linda talking to her sister and was surprised to learn Phillis enjoyed doing laundry also. Linda has gorgeous handwriting. See amazed us all with her ability to write her name with both hands at the same time. The signature written with the left hand was written backwards but when you held it up to a mirror, it was perfect.

Until recently, we spent thirty three years in a 1918 large tudor home. In 1988 when we moved into that home, she went on a search to find a service to assist her in cleaning it. Nobody met her expectations and with very little help she maintained that house immaculately. After retirement, I finally met her expectations where vacuuming of hardwood floors were concerned. (It took a lot of instruction. Everything needs to be covered at least twice. Three times are preferable.) Linda does draw the line occasionally. She doesn't do windows.

Linda handles every task almost effortlessly. Linda is very athletic, especially where balance is concerned. When we were dating, I took her water skiing. I thought I was a pretty hot skier. I didn't know her parents owned a houseboat and they spent virtually every weekend and summer on the lake. She is a fantastic water skier. When the kids were little, we went ice skating. All the kids and I were stumbling all over the rink. Linda took right off and flew around the ring like she had been ice skating from childhood. The same is true of snow skiing.

Linda is a magnificent cook. Her decorating touch is right on. Linda exudes style. She can dress up or down to any occasion with amazing ease. She is a wonderful and talented gardener. One side door garden of our home was her masterpiece. Neighbors and others often complimented her and took pictures. As usual, we did everything together. For birthday or valentine's day, Linda gave me a rose bush and the card said "my little fella". One of the kids or grandkids saw it and the name stuck. I didn't mind. I love being Linda's little fella.

Linda's strength and courage is phenomenal. She displayed this throughout her life especially when she was hit with all the illness and challenges over the most recent years. She amazed us all with the grace and acceptance of her challenges and quietly moved on with life. She maintained that attitude right up until she took her last breath. Over several years, Linda had been facing numerous health challenges. These challenges accelerated dramatically over the past six months with one on top of another. Linda was amazing us all, even the doctors, that she was persevering and seldom complaining. She accepted the diminished quality of life she was given and never complained and made the most of it. My brain was telling me no one can take these multiple abuses to their body and survive. I still had hope, but I realistically couldn't see how she could withstand the challenges thrown at her. On Monday December 18th, 2023, just fifteen days ago, Linda had a doctor's appointment with her surgeon. Her doctor was amazed. She and Linda discussed her improvement and made plans for a second surgery which would allow total recovery. Her doctor couldn't get over the miraculous improvement. Linda had convinced me she was going to totally recover. Linda was invincible.

The amazing fact about all her wonderful strengths is that they never wavered. She was always; kind, loving, caring, strong, loyal, giving, truthful, trusting and I could go on and on. Linda never woke up on the wrong side of the bed. One would think she would slip up occasionally, but while attempting to honor her today, I can't think of a single time during our 62 year marriage she purposely wronged anyone.

Linda is my soulmate. From the day we married and we held hands, I was at home. Linda's touch is magical. When she touched my hand or I touched her shoulder or I put my arm around her waist, her warmth and love fills my soul. Her voice has the same effect on me. Her voice is full of warmth and love. These things haven't lessened over the years but strengthened. Linda puts my soul at peace.

Linda always has my back. When I was a jerk or did something really stupid she didn't waver, she was with me. From the day I married Linda, I became something special. Together we could do anything. I became more confident and assured immediately when Linda Donaldson chose me.

We started our family and all of a sudden we grew up and embarked on a wonderful life of us getting through night school together and going to work for Colgate-Palmolive Company. Although I was the only one officially employed by Colgate, it was our career. I could not have done it without her complete support. In fact, she did far more to keep the family together. I was off working and dining out, etc. while she was getting the kids established in new schools, doctors, churches, and dentists. Colgate moved us six times during our career. Linda never once balked or hesitated, just wanted to know where and when. If it was good for our career, we said yes, if not we both said no.

As I said when I started this conversation of Linda, I want to thank God for creating Linda and allowing us to cross paths. Life with Linda is heaven. Obviously, not everyday was rosey and happy, but even on the darkest days, together we could get through by having each other. The loss of our parents and other close friends was made bearable because we have each other.

I discovered Friday December 22nd, 2023 at approximately 9:15 in the evening, life without Linda is hell. The thought of never being with Linda again was unbearable, hell itself. On that Friday night and Saturday morning, Linda came to me and held my hand. I am aware she is with me now and she has made her presents undeniable. So undeniable that it has saved a wretch like me.

Linda and I were soul mates on this earth. She is my doll baby. I adore everything about her. She is my lil girl, my lil something. She gave me heaven on earth. I had her for my wife for 62 years and 38 days. That isn't enough. We must have more. I don't care if it had been 162 years or 1,062 years it wouldn't be enough. We can't imagine being without each other.

I know there are certain things we as human beings can't wrap our hands around like where does space end and the concept of eternity. Like the song, "I Can Only Imagine", we can only imagine. I came into attempting this honoring, letter, statement, whatever this document is, loving and adoring completely one soul, Linda. Today, I want to shout to the universe and beyond. I adore God and Jesus Christ with every fiber of my being. They have shown me without question, It's all true with no reservations. We will spend eternity together. We will spend eternity with our mothers and fathers. With our children, grandparents, grandchildren. We will spend eternity with our loved ones. I don't know all the details and won't know until I get there. Linda knows. Linda was an angel on earth, and now an angel in heaven.

For those of us left here on earth our grief is tremendous. We react physically to not being able to touch, feel, see and smell Linda. I yearn to hear her sweet voice. The transition from being afraid to go to sleep and having to face the nightmare all over again when I wake, to looking forward to resting and waking each morning with more knowledge and understanding in such a short period of time amazes me. Linda says I haven't seen anything yet. We are all spiritual beings and must go through the process of moving on. The timing of when we depart this earth and join those that have gone before us, is God's will. Until that time, I'm consoled by my doll baby.

Lovingly,

Linda and Howard

TO: OUR GRANDCHILDREN

Ashleigh, Kinsey, Audrey, Shaw, Claudia, Sophia. Jess, Mia, Olivia, Madeleine, Lillian, and Quinnlan

From: Grammy & Granddaddy Subject: Salvation and Everlasting Life

We wanted the opportunity to let you know what has transpired over the past two months in our lives. We had a wonderful life together and would love to do it all over again. This being Valentine's day, it is the first Valentine's day we have spent apart in 63 years. It is especially sensitive that we are physically apart on this special day. It is a sad day for us in this physical world we live in but there are tremendous positives as well. We would love to share the wonderful knowledge and understanding that has been exposed due to Linda's passing.

It's all true! What the Bible says is true! Your soul does not die when you pass on. Through the greatness of the loving God, we can have everlasting life with our loved ones. Through the grace of the Lord, Jesus Christ, and the Holy Spirit we can have eternal life in heaven.

Our parents and grandparents have stressed the teachings of the Bible and directed us towards church and the Lord, but no one ever made us aware of what transpired after a loved one passed on. We would like to share our experiences since December 22nd, 2023. We are extremely close. We are soulmates. I guess we felt we would go out of this world together. Unfortunately, it rarely happens that way. We are all born with an expiration date and the Lord is in control. Whichever one of us that went first, we both felt we would let the other one know all was well. We were right.

This is your grandaddy letting you know from his perspective what has taken place since December 22nd of 2023. Linda and I agree you should be made aware of what has transpired since Linda's passing. The night it happened it was totally unexpected. Linda had a doctor's appointment on Monday, December 18th, and her doctor was amazed she was doing so well. She had completed roughly six weeks of her eight week antibiotic course and the surgeon scheduled her second operation to totally heal the wound. Everything was looking great. Linda had a good day on that Friday. She ate a big lunch around 2:00 PM. She just looked precious after eating and I was playing with her threatening to eat her up and I told her I was going to get all her kisses. She just rolled her eyes at me. I asked her if I could have all her kisses, she answered "sure". Those were the last words we spoke to each other. Linda went to sleep and took an afternoon nap. She slept peacefully from late afternoon until I walked Billy, our dog, at six. She was sleeping so well I let her sleep until Olivia came home from work. Olivia went in to talk to her and she wouldn't wake up. I attempted to wake her and she was warm and relaxed but would not wake up. We called 911 and they were here in minutes while Olivia performed CPR and I went next door to get our neighbor who is a registered nurse. By the time I went to get the neighbor, the paramedics were there. We are two miles from the hospital. I was certain Linda was going to meet this challenge like she had all the others that were thrown at her over the past six months. It was like a nightmare when the paramedic came into the room and advised us Linda had passed. This couldn't be. This is when the nightmare started.

The paramedics left along with the local funeral home and Linda's body. It was surreal, Linda couldn't be gone. I had never been without Linda since we had met when I was seventeen. As the night wore on and the reality of her passing sunk in, I came up with a plan. We were supposed to go together. I will join her. When everyone leaves, I will simply go out into the garage, start the car and leave the door down. This is when she first made me aware of her still being with me. Linda let me know this is the one way we will never be together. It is God's will not ours when we pass on. With this plan out the window, I was forced to face life without Linda. I didn't feel I could, I was asking the Lord to take me. I didn't sleep for the first two or three days. I finally went to sleep and slept about two hours. It was during this sleep that Linda conveyed to me she needed my help with two people and the things she needed help with. One of the people I understood the other I would have never thought of on my own. This gave me a purpose because Linda had asked for my help and I didn't want to let her down. About the same time

I realized I was going to need to tell family and friends about Linda's amazing life.

I still wasn't sleeping but a few hours at a time, I sat down at my laptop and began to attempt to write about our life together. It was going nowhere. I would stare at the computer screen and nothing was happening. Finally, I realized I need to tell people who I am talking about. I wrote, "We are here today to celebrate and I spelled out Linda's entire name; first name, middle name, maiden name, and finally our sir name. A little line appeared perpendicular to the line I was writing on with a little box or flag attached. When I scrolled my mouse across the flag a green box appeared and within this box was written "Linda Sullivan". I didn't know what it was but assumed it was the name I had given the document. This was a new Mac laptop and I had never used a mac before. I ignored the little flag and continued the document. After a long delay I finally thought of something to write on the second line. As I was typing the second line, the first line just disappeared from the page. Poof it was gone. I hadn't highlighted it and hit backspace. The second line was still there. I was confused. What just happened? Again, I sat there for quite a while thinking about what just happened. I decided it was just me being unfamiliar with the apple computer and tried to remember what I had said in the first line. I had just said we were here to celebrate Linda's life and spelled out her entire name. It came to me that Linda never cared a great deal for her middle name. I retyped the sentence leaving out her middle name and no little flag appeared. I still didn't get it but I continued on. These little flags kept appearing from time to time for a couple of days. Since I wasn't sleeping, I would work on it day and night. It kept me from dwelling on the paralyzing grief of life without Linda. About the third day at 4:00 AM, I was writing about how I had virtually forced Linda to elope to

Lafayette, GA with me. The little flags were popping up all over. I ignored them and continued to type. All of a sudden, the entire document disappeared. Gone! It's 4 in the morning and three days and nights of working on this document is gone. I needed help. My computer and phone expert is Olivia. I reluctantly went to Olivia's bedroom and woke her at 4am. She woke up enough to find the document and bring it back to my screen. She informed me I hadn't lost it and handed me back the laptop. Relieved, I returned to my kitchen bar where I was working on the document. I couldn't type or backup. The computer was locked with these little flags sticking up. Reluctantly, I had to go back to Olivia again and wake her up. I could tell she was getting annoyed. She took the computer and laid it on her chest while she tried to fix it. I noticed her eyes opening up and a confused look coming over her face. She said, "It's grammy". She set up in bed and became very excited. She jumped out of bed and began to hug me and exclaim "It's grammy". She carried the computer back to the kitchen bar and pointed out to me that those little flags I was seeing were notifying me I was collaborating with someone on the document. When we scroll the mouse over the flag a green box would pop up with the name "Linda Sullivan". We hugged and rejoiced and woke up the entire house at 4:30 in the morning. I felt like Linda was helping me write this document because I would sit for long periods of time before something would come to me to write about. I was ignorant about what the little flags meant, she had to make the document disappear so Olivia would explain to me she was working with me. Linda left no doubt, she was still with me.

After several minutes of celebrating the knowledge of Linda collaborating with me on this document I settled down to work more on the letter. I went back to the section that caused Linda to make the entire document disappear and removed any reference to the elopement and the flags disappeared. Linda had expressed many years ago she wished we had not eloped because we deprived our parents of the joy of being with us on our wedding day.

Now I knew she was writing it with me and it was flowing much better. Perhaps twenty minutes later, Holly walked into the kitchen and said, "Mom says is". Holly wasn't standing where she could see the screen, she was on the other side of the counter. I didn't understand what she was saying. Holly just kept saying "IS". She finally said, "Mom says you wrote Linda was my soulmate. Mom says Linda is your soulmate". I went back up the page and a couple of paragraphs up the page there was a little flag sticking up where I had typed, "Linda was my soulmate". I changed the was to is and the little flag disappeared.

Linda has come to me several times while I sleep. I wake in the morning clearly understanding what she has conveyed during my sleep. It's always the same, it is accompanied by a warmth that only Linda could give me. It's the same warmth I feel when I hear her voice or she touches me. I awoke one morning with the knowledge I needed to get back in church. I now feel Linda didn't realize I had doubts about the Bible and salvation. I wanted to believe but I had never had that earth shattering eye open- ing revelation other people talk about when they were saved. I think Linda realized when she passed, I wanted to believe but my analytical mind couldn't get by the fact that these things are not possible in our physical world. She has told me I have seen nothing yet, like the song "I Can Only Imagine". By coming back to me and showing me her soul lives on by assisting me on my document celebrating her life she is also telling me, I still have some knowledge to gain. I told Glen and Susie I wanted to start going back to church. I had always been somewhat of a roadblock to Linda keeping us in church and Bible study. They agreed and told me about a couple of local churches. Two of them were right across the street from each other about four miles away. Glen seemed to prefer The Christ Church over The Hope Church. The first week we went to The Christ Church. I had never been to either church. I mistakenly turned into The Hope Church. I had to back out and go across the street. Something told me you should be going to the Hope Church. I enjoyed the service at the Christ Church but it didn't really answer any questions for me. Glen said he really enjoyed the service and minister. I still felt like the other church was calling me. They agreed we would try The Hope Church the next week. We all went to The Hope Church the following week and it was amazing. I feel like Linda with the grace of God, Jesus and the Holy Spirit led me to this church, on that particular Sunday, to hear that sermon, from that minister. We were all raw because it was so close to Linda's passing but so were we the previous week. The minister prefaced the sermon with the statement the next five to seven minutes of the Bible changed his life (John 14). It was scripture about the last supper when Jesus is to be crucified the next day and the disciples are wanting to go with him. Jesus tells them they can't as they have much more work to be done on earth. It is God's will when they leave this world not man's. Jesus tells them they will do much more than him here on earth. The disciples question him on how are we to do this if you are gone. Jesus tells them the Lord will send them the comforter or Holy Spirit to guide them. Jesus goes on to tell them the Holy Spirit can't guide or help them unless you let him into your soul. This is the part I didn't recognize or understand. I had never understood the necessity of letting the Holy Spirit into your soul. I opened my heart and soul to the Holy Spirit and it was a revelation. It was as a light went on, it was never about what you couldn't do but what you can do. With the Holy Spirit guiding us we won't even think about doing evil things but rather think about all the good we can do in this world. Our job here on earth is to witness God's love and mercy through our actions and how we treat our fellow man. To be a disciple of God's word and teaching and convert as many as possible away from the dark one and to God. We will have to wait and hear Linda's amazing revelation of what has transpired since December 22nd 2023. She is telling me not to feel sorry for her because she can't go to Panera Bread and get cheddar soup. She tells me I haven't seen anything yet.

This is why we are writing this letter to you. We want to be with you everlastingly. We want to make it as easy as possible to believe God's word. No human is without sin but God gave his only son so that we could have everlasting life. Just that word, "everlasting" is inconceivable to our worldly minds. Our small minds have difficulty getting around concepts like forever and timeless. Things like where does space end and the concept of nothing. The Bible says all will be revealed to us and I believe it will. I know Linda is with me. I feel her warmth. I yearn to be with her completely but she has made it possible for me to carry on and do God's will until he calls me home. We love you all and thank God for allowing you to bless our lives. If you remember Grammy didn't like to say goodbye, Linda always said.

See ya,
Grammy and Granddaddy

CLOSING THOUGHT FROM THE AUTHORS

It has now been almost ten months since Linda passed. Please notice that we did write "Authors" not just Author. This is what prompted the attempt to write a book. Linda and I wrote this book together after her passing. I am convinced she had more input than I did. Just as in life, she was the wiser and always headed us in the right direction. As our son Glen once told me, "Dad you were never in control".

This has been one of the most difficult yet soul searching experiences of my life and I think I could say of our lives. I should have bought stock in "Kleenex" before we started to write. And the saga continues. She is still with me and giving me the will to complete God's wonderful life he has afforded us. One of the biggest ways she has supported me is to document it and put it in writing to help everyone when they are facing physical separation from their loved one.

We have discovered through the attempt to get the book published, it is a long and time consuming process. It has forced you to read and reread the thoughts you have put on paper. When you reread what you wrote, you are forced to relive it, more Kleenex. But very sweet and loving memories. It has given us the opportunity and time to call on a host of family and friends in writing the book. Their input has been wonderful.

I was walking my little pack of three dogs this morning and feeling very sad and lonely. As usual these days, I can't help but tear up when reminiscing about our lives together and while walking the puppies on a pretty sunny day and thinking, Linda would have loved this day. I had my sunglasses on. One of the pups pooped and I was attempting to pick it up but I couldn't see. As I was bending over, the tears had fallen on my sunglasses. The dogs had done their deed and were ready to move on. They were pulling as I attempted to take one of my tissues out of my pocket to clear the tears on my glasses. That's when it hit me. What are you crying about? That's when all the writing and rewriting combined with all the input from family and friends made me realize I was the luckiest man on God's green earth. I would like to acknowledge some of those that helped get me to that realization. Perhaps Linda had already come to that conclusion.

Both my sisters helped me a great deal. Wanda was the one that told me after Linda passed, "I don't feel sorry for you one bit. How many people have what you and Linda have? Not many." Barbara proof read my manuscript and told me my epilogue was much too long. Both gave me tremendous encouragement. Several close friends in the neighborhood read it and gave me positive and negative feedback. The publisher gave me good constructive feedback. One of the most impactful feedbacks we received was from someone neither one of us ever met or knew. It was the next door neighbor to Glen and Susie, my son and his wife. Susie had read the manuscript and asked if her next door neighbor could read it. Obviously, we didn't mind. It could be helpful to get feedback from someone that had never met us. Her neighbor's response surprised me. She thought it was a love letter. She then followed that up with, "Did she know how much he loved her"? Susie responded with, "Absolutely, and it went both ways".

The delay in getting this book published has had the positive effect of having to review and reminisce our lives together. To have this total stranger verify our writing about our life together and Linda's passing seemed like a long love letter, opened my eyes. It pretty much sums up our life together, a long love affair. God has blessed us to have found each other, lived the life dreams are made of, and parted with our last words to each other, "Can I have all your kisses?" "Sure!"

It has now been almost eleven months since Linda's passing. We don't want to confuse anyone but we are inserting this paragraph roughly one month after finishing the book. My publisher called last week and told me he would have the "Proof Copy" of our book. It is an actual complete book of what the final book will look like. If we approve it, it will go to print and become available at numerous book retailers. He was available Thursday, a week later. As we sat there at our usual meeting place, Starbucks at Liberty Mall, and discussed the book we eventually came to the conclusion, this book is completed. I looked at my publisher and said, "I guess you want some money". He agreed that would be nice. As I began to write the check, I needed to date the check.

Since starting this journey to write and publish this book, I have little need of the date other than to pay my bills on time. It was a Thursday and we were meeting on a Thursday in November. He responded with November the 14th. WOW! It's our anniversary. I had let our anniversary slip up on me. I had thought about it coming up several times but once I learned our finished book was going to be delivered on the next Thursday, I anticipated nothing else but seeing our finished book. What an anniversary gift, our finished book was delivered on our sixty-third wedding anniversary. I couldn't help it. I teared up. My publisher seemed to understand. Perhaps irony, but I prefer to believe my baby is still with me and we received our published book on our special day.

We would like to leave you with something Linda adopted and practiced throughout her adult life. She would not end a conversation with goodbye. It was just too final. She shortened "See you later" to "See Ya". Virtually, everyone in the family has adopted the practice.

See Ya